JESUS IN THE HOUSE

Jesus
in the
House

Gospel
Reflections
on
Christ's
Presence
in
the
Home

ALLAN F. WRIGHT

ST. ANTHONY MESSENGER PRESS
Cincinnati, Ohio

Cover and book design by Mark Sullivan
Cover image: istockphoto.com/Andy Hill

LIBRARY OF CONGRESS CATALOGING-IN-PUBLICATION DATA

Wright, Allan F., 1964-
Jesus in the house : Gospel reflections on Christ's presence in the home / Allan F. Wright.
p. cm.
Includes bibliographical references.
ISBN-13: 978-0-86716-791-7 (pbk. : alk. paper) 1. Home—Religious aspects—Catholic Church—Meditations. 2. Family—Religious aspects—Catholic Church—Meditations. 3. Bible. N.T. Gospels—Meditations. 4. Jesus Christ—Meditations. 5. Catholic Church—Prayer-books and devotions—English. I. Title.

BX2351.W74 2007
248.4'82—dc22

2006038493

ISBN 978-0-86716-791-7

Published by St. Anthony Messenger Press
28 W. Liberty St.
Cincinnati, OH 45202
www.AmericanCatholic.org

Printed in the United States of America.

Printed on acid-free paper.

07 08 09 10 5 4 3 2 1

To Desiree and Sophia,
Joy upon Joy!

CONTENTS

ACKNOWLEDGMENTS

TO MY MOM AND DAD, WHO RAISED US IN THE HOME, AROUND THE TABLE and where we still gather today to talk, eat and laugh. To my brother David and his wife Diane, who are a blessing to our family. For my sister Nina, one of the strongest people I know, who has sacrificed her life and everything she does for her family, and to her husband, Todd. To Christopher my nephew and companion on many adventures, who has made being an uncle one of the joys of my life, and to his younger brother, Charlie, who has many adventures before him! To my niece Cheri, who has grown so much in the past year that I can't wait to see what's next. To the Matchen family, Monroe, Paula, Jordan and Kelsey, and the Rejcek family, for always making me feel right at home in the great state of Texas. In appreciation to Amber Dolle, who is an affirming voice and always takes the time to "look things over" for me. To Nick Dolle for his ever-inspiring "Aggie" spirit. To the Union Catholic community and especially Sister Percylee Hart, R.S.M., who is a constant source of encouragement, vision and faith. To Sister Catherine Carroll and Kathy Grausam and the religion department, for their years of faith and witness laboring for teenagers and for putting up with me over the years at U.C. Heartfelt thanks to Father Dennis Berry, S.T., Father Kent Weidie, S.T., and especially to Sister Gail Lambert, M.S.B.T., whose missionary witness to the Young Adult Community at the Father Judge

Apostolic Center touched all who entered. For Mike and Cary St. Pierre, partners in ministry and faithful friends during the peaks and valleys of life. To Dr. James Sulliman, for his friendship and fidelity to the Catholic faith. For Roger and Sandy Wilkin, for always welcoming me as part of their family from the Young Life days to our present collaboration with Apostolic Connections. To Sister Mary Joseph Schultz, S.C.C., and the wonderful community at Assumption College for Sisters and those who study there, your generosity and hospitality to me and my family always refreshes and renews me. Thanks to Father John Morley for his years of friendship and hospitality. To Dianne Traflet, J.D., S.T.D., and Diane Carr, for their support and encouragement and their labor at Immaculate Conception Seminary Institute for Christian Spirituality. To Bishop Serratelli, S.T.D., S.S.L., D.D., for instilling in me a greater love of Christ through Scripture. To Reverend Harold Drexler whose insights into Christ's love for families was a motivating factor in writing this book. To Monsignor Patrick Brown, pastor of the most "family friendly" parish I know. To the Missionaries of Charity (Contemplative) in Plainfield, New Jersey—your joy and love for Jesus and Mary and hospitality to my family strengthens and renews me more than you'll ever know. In appreciation of the work of my editor, Abby Colich, and for all the care given to me at every turn by those who work at St. Anthony Messenger Press. In memory of Stephen Demcsak, faithful friend, who had a way of making people feel at home wherever he was. In appreciation to all the wonderful Texas barbeque joints, where the glorious consumption of brisket and steak may perhaps be a foreshadowing of the great eschatological banquet in heaven.

Sentire

Cum

Ecclesia

FOREWORD

WHEN POPE JOHN PAUL II CAME TO THE UNITED STATES AND CELEBRATED Mass at Giants Stadium, he spoke about the family, "as a vocation, to be a place where people are loved not for what they say or do, but simply because they were born." Author Allan Wright has taken the words of the sacred Scriptures and has reinterpreted the gift of family life with the teachings of Christianity.

The family is the privileged setting where every person learns to give and receive love. That is why the church constantly wishes to demonstrate her pastoral concern for this reality, so basic for the human person. This is what she teaches in her magisterium: "God who is love and who created man and woman for love has called them to love. By creating man and woman he called them to an intimate communion of life and love in marriage. 'So that they are no longer two, but one flesh' (Matthew 19:6)" (*Compendium of the Catechism of the Catholic Church*, 337).[1]

The family is an intermediate institution between individuals and society, and nothing can completely take its place. The family is itself based primarily on a deep interpersonal relationship between husband and wife, sustained by affection and mutual understanding. To enable this, it receives abundant help from God in the sacrament of matrimony, which brings with it a true vocation to holiness. Would that our children might experience more the harmony and affection between their parents, rather than disagreements and discord, since the love between father and mother is a source of great security for children and it teaches them the beauty of a faithful and lasting love.

Wright explains that the family is a necessary good for peoples, an indispensable foundation for society and a great and lifelong treasure for couples. It is a unique good for children, who are meant to be the fruit of the love, of the total and generous self-giving of their parents. To proclaim the whole truth about the family based on marriage as a domestic church and a sanctuary of life is a great responsibility incumbent upon all.

Scripture answers the challenges of present-day society, marked by the centrifugal forces generated especially in urban settings, making it necessary to ensure that families do not feel alone. A small family can encounter difficult obstacles when it is isolated from relatives and friends. The ecclesial community therefore has the responsibility of offering support, encouragement and spiritual nourishment, which can strengthen the cohesiveness of the family, especially in times of trial or difficulty.

Christ has shown us what is always to be the supreme source of our life and thus of the lives of families: "This is my commandment, that you love one another as I have loved you. No one has greater love than this, to lay down one's life for one's friends" (John 15:13). The love of God himself has been poured out upon us in baptism. Consequently, families are called to experience this same kind of love, for the Lord makes it possible for us, through our human love, to be as sensitive, loving and merciful as Christ.

Together with passing on the faith and the love of God, one of the greatest responsibilities of families is that of training free and responsible persons. For this reason parents need to give their children greater freedom gradually, while remaining for some time the guardians of that freedom. If children see that their parents—and, more generally, all the adults around them—

live life with joy and enthusiasm, despite all difficulties, they will themselves develop that profound "joy of life," which can help them to overcome wisely the inevitable obstacles and problems that are part of life. Furthermore, when families are not closed in on themselves, children come to learn that every person is worthy of love, and that there is a basic, universal brotherhood which embraces every human being.

Wright clearly helps us see that children need to be brought up in the faith, to be loved and protected. Along with their basic right to be born and to be raised in the faith, children also have the right to a home where the sacred Word of God is taken as its model, and to be shielded from all dangers and threats.

Monsignor Patrick Brown
Pastor, St. Vincent De Paul Church,
Stirling, New Jersey
Feast of the Little Flower,
October 1, 2006

INTRODUCTION

SO OFTEN WHEN I REFLECT ON THE MISSION AND MINISTRY OF JESUS Christ, my mind conjures up an image of Jesus out and about among the people, walking the dusty roads of the Middle East with his band of disciples, teaching and preaching the Good News. It's a satisfying image and one, no doubt, that happened often in and around Nazareth, Capernaum, Jerusalem and throughout the land of Israel. Upon further reflection and reading of the Gospel accounts of Jesus' life, I have been pleasantly surprised by how often Jesus' teaching, forgiving, eating and healing takes place not in the open air, but, more often than not, in the home. In describing the nature of the kingdom, Jesus employed examples from household, family and domestic life. Why did Jesus spend so much time in the homes and houses of the people? How did Jesus' own experience of home assist in his formation throughout his childhood and facilitate his understanding of the importance of home?

More importantly, what lessons are there for us? Certainly Jesus had a powerful impact in the homes he entered to heal, share meals, teach and forgive. Are our homes much different? Do we still need the presence of Jesus in our homes today? How much different would our homes be today if we taught, forgave, healed and shared meals as Jesus did? Is the home still a place where the most important lessons of life are both taught and caught? I tend to think yes, they are.

In reflecting upon my own experience of *home,* I can honestly say that it has formed me into the person I am today more so than any other experience or influence. I have had the opportunity to study, vacation and share meals with people overseas in Paris, London, Prague, Istanbul, Krakow, Jerusalem and in fancy restaurants as well as humble barbeque joints and diners across the United States. None of those experiences, however, have taught me the important lessons that I've learned and the sense of family that I recall so vividly today. Gathering around the red circular dining room table for dinner each evening in our home on Central Avenue, we shared not only my mom's wonderful home-cooked meals, but it was also a place where the experiences of life were shared. Homework was completed and art projects glued together. We absorbed the daily news our parents discussed. On rare occasions when the TV was allowed to be turned on, we laughed at the humor of *The Uncle Floyd Show* or tuned into a must-see sporting event that brought us together. The sense of humor that my family enjoys was fine-tuned around that table as we tried to surpass each other with clever puns and retold the same jokes over and over again. The grandkids are presently learning those same jokes around that same table.

The important lessons of forgiveness and teaching were more caught than taught by living in my family. I recall one time when my mom made me go back to a friend's house and apologize to a friend's mother for something one of my other buddies did while playing hockey. It was not I who was in the wrong but my friend, mind you, but because I had invited him to play, his bad behavior was now my problem, too. That was one of the longest quarter-mile walks I have ever made in my life, but the lesson concerning the importance of forgiveness and accountability has stayed with me through the years. Simple gestures of writing thank-you notes, showing gratitude and being accountable was lived out daily in our household and continues to impact my brother, sister and me today.

Home for me was and is a place of stability and unconditional love where we had boundaries and the freedom to be all God called us to be. I knew right from wrong not from lectures but from example. When I had the opportunity to choose right or wrong, more often than not I did the right thing, not from a sense of fear but from the fact that I did not want to dishonor my family. I think that explains a lot about who I am today.

A phrase that my good friend Reverend Harold Drexler has repeated to me on numerous occasions is this, "Touch a person and you touch a family." When one family member suffers, the whole family is concerned and affected. When the family member is restored to good health or the crisis is over, the entire family breathes a little easier. When Jesus healed an individual, he healed a family. When Jesus taught, his teaching impacted a family. When Jesus ate a meal, he did so in the home, which therefore influenced a family. When Jesus announced good news to a person, that person went back and shared it with his family. What a difference the presence of Jesus had, and continues to have, in the home and on families.

Thirty times the word *home* is used in the Gospels, and the word *house* is used ninety-nine times (forty-three times in Luke) in the *New Revised Standard Version* of the Bible. Those numbers are striking considering that there are only a total of eighty-nine chapters in the four Gospels combined. It is obvious from the numbers alone that Jesus spent a great deal of time in the home with families. If it was important to him, it should be important to us.

While speaking to the parents of my students and to adults interested in Christian formation, I often find that they feel uncomfortable and ill-equipped to engage in matters of faith in the home and engaging others in matters of faith. Perhaps the subject of faith was not discussed in their homes growing up or they just feel inadequate in doing so. Whatever the reason, this book is designed to help you get the conversations started and to give you ideas that will help start making an immediate impact in your home. It is designed for use by individuals, families or small groups.

I've taught at the Father Judge Center for Young Adults in New Jersey for over ten years and as good as I may be at opening up and sharing the Word of God with them, what I have found to be most fruitful is to speak less and allow more time for people to speak to one another. This is accomplished by making my scriptural point in less than fifteen minutes and then asking the gathered participants to break into groups of four or five and invite them to share some thoughts on the questions I have provided. We then regroup, and if anyone wants to share an insight with the larger group they can. The problem is never getting them to talk, but rather, getting them back together.

In the same way, my wife belongs to an informal mom's group that meets once a week in the morning for a few hours. Children and babies are present at their meetings, so it can be challenging to be focused and enter into a contemplative mindset. However, these moms take the time, in the midst of the nursing, changing diapers and giving out snacks, to share their experiences and respond to questions. They read a chapter of a book beforehand, and when they meet, they go around the room and just start sharing. I'm told that they rarely get beyond the first two questions, but that's all right. The very act of sharing allows the Holy Spirit to open them up to each other and to God. I have included some practical steps in starting and running a small group after the following section about the house church in early Christianity.

A BRIEF SKETCH OF THE HOUSE CHURCH IN EARLY CHRISTIANITY

ONE OF THE THINGS MY WIFE AND I OFTEN DO WHILE TRAVELING through a major city is to stop and visit the local shrine or cathedral, say a prayer, light a candle and marvel at the architecture and beauty of the worship space. There is much to be said about the peaceful atmosphere that a beautiful church can create. The space literally communicates the presence of God.

It was not always this way in the history of the Christian church, however. Archaeologists tell us that the first actual church building is to be found at Dura Europos on the Euphrates, dating approximately from the year 231.

The earliest Christians did not have church buildings as we know them today. They gathered together at individual homes for worship, *agape* (or *love feasts*) and celebrating the Eucharist. Saint Paul makes mention of this in 1 Corinthians 11:17–33. The word that we use to translate *church* is the Greek word *ecclesia*, which translates as *assembly*, or *gathering*. Eventually these homes were converted into full-time churches, or *domus ecclesiae*.

In 1 Corinthians 11:23 Saint Paul makes note that he received the teaching about the Eucharist "from the Lord." It was not in a private revelation or personal appearance from Jesus that he learned the tradition of the Eucharist. Rather, it was from a living, vibrant Christian community in which the Lord was fully alive, active and present. He is still present today wherever the community is gathered and the Eucharist is celebrated.

What did these early Christian house churches look like? The followers of Jesus likely gathered in the home of a wealthy patron who had room to spare. Saint Paul mentions both men and women who opened their homes; most likely they were owners of large homes, as hosts of early church gatherings. Due to the fact that even new synagogues grew out of Jewish communities that first gathered in the home, the early church would have had some model to follow.

It's also important to note, as I have already suggested, that Jesus spent a great deal of his time in homes. All four Gospels attest to the fact that Jesus spent many hours sharing meals within the home; some of the most notable include the banquet in the house of Levi, the supper in Simon the Pharisee's home where Jesus was denied hospitality, the welcome of Mary and Martha, the meal with the tax collector Zacchaeus, the Passover meal in which Jesus instituted the Eucharist and the breaking of bread at Emmaus after the resurrection of Jesus. If the home is where Jesus met with people and taught, healed, forgave and shared meals, the early Christian followers would have had the supreme model to follow.

In the Middle East sharing a meal together is viewed much differently than in the West. Middle Eastern culture informs us that food is not only for mere sustenance but it reveals your relationship to the one who has invited you and to your standing in the community. Even today in these countries, accepting a meal invitation relays the message that you accept your host as an equal. Likewise, declining such an invitation is a great insult that suggests that the host is not worthy of your presence. This "dishonoring" of the host has serious social consequences, which could have led to conflict and century-long hostilities.

Jesus invited all around the table to share in this dining fellowship. By inviting everyone he was proclaiming that no one is outside the scope of God's love. Isaiah looked forward to a time where "all peoples" would be gathered around the table. "On this mountain the LORD of hosts will make for all peoples / a feast of rich food, a feast of well-aged wines, / of rich food filled with marrow, of well-aged wines strained clear" (Isaiah 25:6). Jesus ushered in this messianic moment by sharing meals around a table in the home.

Saint Paul mentions that some people bring a prayer or a song when they gather together. Others bring prophecies or charismatic gifts to the table. So whether the gift is food or an outward sign of piety, the whole community contributes to the service.

The Pauline Epistles acquaint us with individuals who opened their homes for Christian worship and were leaders in the local communities:

- Priscilla and Aquila in Ephesus; Acts 18:1–26; Romans 16:3–5; and 1 Corinthians 16:19: "The churches of Asia send greetings. Aquila and Prisca, together with the church in their house, greet you warmly in the Lord."
- Philemon in Colossae; Philemon 1:2: "...to Apphia our sister, to Archippus our fellow soldier, and to the church in your house...."
- Nympha in Laodicea; Colossians 4:15: "Give my greetings to the brothers and sisters in Laodicea, and to Nympha and the church in her house."

Saint Paul formed and wrote to these small Christian communities who gathered in house churches. A closer examination of these letters reveals the love Saint Paul had for them and the love they were to show to each other. As in any household there are problems and jealousies, which are to be expected. Saint Paul's letters were often an attempt to show the emerging communities a better way of living with each other and living as a Christian in the world, the way of love. Love is not defined as a feeling or emotion, but love is defined in the person of Jesus. The early Christian house churches struggled to live out their faith in a world that experienced division, war, prejudice, sexism, envy and a host of other problems—just like we do today. Saint Paul was not the director of evangelization (the Holy Spirit has that job), but Saint

Paul was certainly bold, loving and wise as he formed those communities and as he lived out the faith in the providence of his everyday life.

What wisdom can we glean from the way the early church operated? I think the lessons are many. For example, when I was younger and involved in running retreats or doing things in ministry, I was always thinking "big." While it's good to think big, when it comes to how you get there, it always needs to starts small and start with people. Big events, conferences and meetings are fine, although, if you don't make significant contact with a few committed people, the lights will go out and much activity will have taken place without much being accomplished.

I'm not talking about getting rid of large churches; they are where the Catholic community gathers together in all of its diversity and beauty to celebrate the Eucharist. Meeting in a house as a small community, however, can bring about changes and conversion that rarely occur by gathering for Eucharist once a week. Like the early disciples who devoted themselves to "the apostles' teaching and fellowship, to the breaking of bread and the prayers" (Acts 2:42), we, too, tend to grow more in our faith when we gather in small groups to break open the Word of God, reflect upon the teachings of the church, writings of the saints, various encyclicals and church documents and share our lives with a few trusted people.

The small group can present an opportunity for deep sharing to take place. It can also offer an environment in which groups of individuals can experience the grace of fellowship and, together, pray for God's will to be done. Like the early Christian communities, the home is often where the exchange of faith occurs.

HOW A SMALL FAITH-SHARING GROUP SHOULD FUNCTION

WHAT DOES SUCH A SMALL GROUP ACTUALLY LOOK LIKE? IT MAY BE EASY to assume that most people have participated in a small group of some kind at work, school or in one's parish, but it's better not to assume that one knows how a small group properly functions. The following are some basic principles for small group meetings.

• Begin with a time for mingling and light refreshments.
• Let the group members know the schedule for the evening and that they should be respectful of people's time.
• Start light, go deeper. It's that simple. Don't sit down, look at the person sitting across from you and ask, "So what's the biggest sin you committed this week?" In other words, don't start off with deep or vulnerable questions that could close doors before you even get to the front porch. Start with ice-breaker questions such as: What is your name? Where did you grow up? What's your favorite type of food? I've never met a person who felt intimidated by those nonthreatening questions. Bring up something fun to share, and the participants will have answered the easy questions and have a positive momentum going toward sharing answers.
• If the small group is functioning correctly, members will feel comfortable, safe and eager to proceed into deeper conversations. At this point slowly go deeper with the questions, eventually maybe getting even more personal and more toward the heart of the topic of faith. In the following example of a small group meeting discussion, you can see how the questions progress:

    1. Share your name and favorite type of food. (After the people in the group feel comfortable with one another, these questions can be dropped. If you are creative, it can be a fun way of finding new things about old friends!)

9

2. Read Luke 2:48–52 aloud.

3. Questions for discussion:

- Who has influenced you in your faith life? Was it one person or a number of people who helped form you?
- Jesus is in the temple, asking questions and listening. How do you put yourself in a position to listen to God or learn about your faith?
- What things do you think God treasures about you and writes down in his book?
- What experiences have formed your faith in the home?

4. Close with a prayer.

- Know the purpose of your group. Frequently I ask youth workers what their purpose is for small groups. Many of them have trouble answering this question. Is your purpose informational? By informational, I mean, do you want to provide a venue in which people can learn the material in a way other than from a textbook? If this is the case, your focus would be the information at hand. Is your purpose relational and aimed at deepening the relationships in the group? If so, your focus would be on providing a discussion that would motivate group members to open up and share their experiences with each other. By providing the appropriate type of environment for the group, you are helping to increase each individual's level of trust and the vulnerability that they will allow.

- Listen to others. It's simple...it's basic...but it's often neglected, and it's one of the most important reasons for even having a small group and vital to its existence. People want to feel heard! Allow an opportunity for each group member to open up, share their thoughts and truly feel heard. Notice I didn't say "be heard" but "feel heard." This is not just a case of repeating back what was said or smiling in the speaker's direction. Rather, this is empathetic listening in which others really attempt to "feel" what the person is saying. So often I am ready to reply before the person I'm supposed to be listening to is finished speaking. However, more times than not, the individual speaking doesn't need my mouth to provide an "answer," but rather my ears and heart to simply listen. This is a skill anyone can acquire with practice and patience.

- Keep the group to a small, workable size. This last small group basic instruction is not only an observation, but it is also a fact. As the group size grows, impact shrivels. The more people in a group equals the less amount of time each individual has to be heard. As the group size gets bigger, trust in the group gets smaller, and people will open up less. The less people open up, the less they will grow. (When I speak to groups of twenty or more, I always try to have them break into smaller groups if only for a few questions.)

- Don't be upset with the person who says nothing or seems to be resisting you. Those individuals are precisely the ones we should pay most attention to. Pray for them. Don't be afraid to follow up one-on-one with them afterward. My experience as a teacher has shown me that some students are more reflective and need more time to process the information they receive. Also, silence does not necessarily equal a lack of involvement or concern. We don't have to pray out loud in order for God to hear us. Learn to be comfortable with silence. Remember, you care about each group member because it is our duty to care, regardless of whether they respond to Christ or not. They may not remember the words you spoke in the small group but they will remember that you cared for them. Always remember, small groups are about people—not programs.

With these thoughts in mind consider starting a small Christian community or sharing group at your parish, or better yet, in your home.

ABOUT THE FORMAT OF THIS BOOK

EACH CHAPTER BEGINS WITH A GOSPEL STORY INVOLVING JESUS' PRESENCE in the home followed by my commentary on that story, which may include reflection, anecdotes and putting the story into historical context. I have included a prayer in order for you to prayerfully reflect on the Good News God has so graciously given to us. I encourage you to pray your own prayer in addition to mine.

At the end of each chapter I offer a quote from one of the documents of the church, a saint or holy individual, or an ordinary person whose thoughts on the themes of sharing meals, healing, teaching and forgiveness I feel are relevant to living out the message today. Also included at the end of each chapter are reflection questions, especially important for small groups, as well as "Chapter Challenges," which will enable you to put your faith into practice today. Feel free to improve on any of them or make up your own challenges as a family.

It is my prayer that you will use this book as a way of introducing a growing faith into your home, with your friends and with small faith-sharing groups. I offer these reflections as a way of entering into the story and taking a seat, if you will, in the homes where Jesus was present. We are invited not just to read the Scriptures as we would a novel, but to enter into them with our hearts, minds and senses, to close our eyes and imagine ourselves present. The preparations have been made, the door is open...enter in.

No eye has seen, nor ear heard,
    nor the human heart conceived,
what God has prepared for those who love him.
(1 Corinthians 2:9)

Allan F. Wright
Feast of the Holy Family, 2005

ONE

A Home Welcomes New Life
(Luke 1:39–56)

In those days Mary set out and went with haste to a Judean town in the hill country, *where she entered the house of Zechariah and greeted Elizabeth.* When Elizabeth heard Mary's greeting, the child leaped in her womb. And Elizabeth was filled with the Holy Spirit and exclaimed with a loud cry, "Blessed are you among women, and blessed is the fruit of your womb. And why has this happened to me, that the mother of my Lord comes to me? For as soon as I heard the sound of your greeting, the child in my womb leaped for joy. And blessed is she who believed that there would be a fulfillment of what was spoken to her by the Lord."

And Mary said,

"My soul magnifies the Lord,
  and my spirit rejoices in God my Savior,
for he has looked with favor on the lowliness of his
  servant.

Surely, from now on all generations will call me blessed;
for the Mighty One has done great things for me,
  and holy is his name.

His mercy is for those who fear him
from generation to generation.
He has shown strength with his arm;
he has scattered the proud in the thoughts of their hearts.
He has brought down the powerful from their thrones,
and lifted up the lowly;
he has filled the hungry with good things,
and sent the rich away empty.
He has helped his servant Israel,
in remembrance of his mercy,
according to the promise he made to our ancestors,
to Abraham and to his descendants forever."
And Mary remained with her about three months and then returned to her home.

IN ALL OF THE BOOKS OF THE NEW TESTAMENT, ONLY LUKE AND MATTHEW record any mention of the birth story of Jesus. Saints Mark, John, Paul, Peter and the other authors apparently felt no need to go back to this event. It was important, however, in the mind of Luke and Matthew to go back to the beginning, before the miracles, before the preaching, before the joy and the suffering. The story begins in a home, a home of friends and family.

I am often taken aback that these familiar and beautiful words said by Elizabeth and Mary are spoken in a home, a simple, most likely peasant, home. Not in a cathedral or palace, nor a castle or mansion worthy of a wealthy person, but a simple house. How often has this Magnificat been beautifully sung and proclaimed throughout the world, through the ages? How many artists have crafted statues, paintings, frescoes and stained-glass windows in honor of Mary as she speaks the words, "My soul magnifies the Lord..."? These beautiful words were first spoken in a home.

The home of Zechariah and Elizabeth was a house that must have felt partially empty. Earlier on in the story we are told that Elizabeth was barren. For a Jewish couple of the time having no children was distressing and meant that they would have no future descendants and no children to look after them in their old age. Children are a blessing from God, yet Zechariah and Elizabeth, who are faithful to God, remain childless. Uncertainties about God's will or questions about whether or not they had offended God may have entered their thoughts. Couples today who find it difficult to conceive may also struggle with the "why us" questions that Zechariah and Elizabeth may

✢ ✢ ✢

"CONCERN FOR THE CHILD, EVEN BEFORE BIRTH, FROM THE FIRST MOMENT OF CONCEPTION AND THEN THROUGHOUT THE YEARS OF INFANCY AND YOUTH, IS THE PRIMARY AND FUNDAMENTAL TEST OF THE RELATIONSHIP OF ONE HUMAN BEING TO ANOTHER."
—Pope John Paul II,
Familiaris Consortio[2]

have entertained. Seeking God's will together in prayer may certainly be a unifying force and ease some of the pain that may accompany those questions. This reality did not shake the faith that Elizabeth and Zechariah had in God because "both of them were righteous before God, living blameless according to all the commandments and regulations of the Lord" (Luke 1:6). Zechariah is in the midst of performing his priestly duties when the angel appears to him and announces that his prayer has been heard. When the angel of the Lord says, "Your prayer has been heard," we know they must have put this matter before God in prayer. They had not given up on God and God's providence and timing. God had certainly not given up on them.

The joy and anticipation of a new child that was evidenced in Zechariah and Elizabeth's house was elevated by Mary's presence. This was an eighty- to one-hundred-mile journey for Mary, taking three or four days to complete. What a gift it must have been to have Mary present in the home. What did the greeting of Mary sound like? Did she knock on the door and say, "shalom," "peace"? Did she call out a name or perhaps say, "Do not be afraid, it is I"? Whatever the greeting, Mary's presence was an occasion for great joy. Imagine the excitement of Elizabeth, so much so that the child "leaped in her womb."

When was the last time Mary had seen Elizabeth? Was Elizabeth glowing with joy? After six months was her pregnancy showing? I imagine them both sitting down and saying to each other at the same time, "you are not going to believe what has happened to me since I saw you last!" They laugh and then begin to tell each other of the things God has done, both amazed at God's mercy and love. Being a man makes this event a little difficult to imagine or to enter into, but as a father I recall thrilling times during my wife's pregnancy when our daughter Sophia was making her presence known by leaps, elbows and kicks. I imagine the joy and anticipation must have been similar for both Joseph and Zechariah.

The first words we hear Mary say are, "My soul magnifies the Lord...." Her first thoughts are of God as she shares her good news and then begins to sing out her song of praise to God who has looked favorably on the lowliness of his servant. The praise of God resounds throughout the house in the presence of family. What a wonderful image of home, a home where family is welcomed, new life is respected and God is honored.

As any couple who has become pregnant can attest, this is not an isolated joy. Phone calls are made to parents who are now grandparents, to brothers and sisters who are now aunts and uncles and to cousins and friends and coworkers. The whole family is affected and shares in the joy with the couple.

The good news of Mary's conception of Jesus includes you and me as well. For we are a part of the family of God; we are redeemed by the saving work of Jesus on the cross that began with Mary's "yes" to God. The Scripture reveals that after three months Mary returned to her home. Good news shared first in the house of a relative was then shared at her own home. What glorious changes she would experience and witness both inside and outside the womb. Mary was present from beginning to end, from the womb to the tomb and beyond. We can bring Mary's example of joy and praise into our homes and honor her by honoring Jesus. We can make our homes a welcoming place where good news is shared. With the example of Mary going back home we, too, one day will "go home" to be with God, who loves us from the beginning and all through our journey on earth.

PRAYER

Loving God and Father, we praise you for the gift of life from conception to natural death. Give us a greater appreciation and respect for life, especially the unborn, and for families and homes to be open to the gift of life. Open our eyes and give us the strength we need to nurture and support life in our homes, families and communities. Guard us from ever harming human life and give us the fortitude and courage to stand up for life when it's attacked. Protect women who are pregnant. Provide them the support and joy that Mary and Elizabeth received in their homes. Open our hearts and the doors of our homes to those who may be in need spiritually, emotionally, psychologically and financially that we may welcome and be as generous to them as we would be to you. We ask this in Jesus' name, under the protection of Mary, Mother of God, and Mother of the church. Amen.

REFLECTION QUESTIONS

1. Can you think of homes you have entered in which you have experienced hospitality and welcome like Mary experienced? What stands out about those homes?

2. How is your home a welcoming place? Do people feel comfortable in your home as Mary must have been welcomed and loved in Zechariah and Elizabeth's house?

3. What are some of the qualities that make a home a Christian home?

4. How are Jesus and Mary present and welcomed in your home today?

CHAPTER CHALLENGES

* I will write a note of support and encouragement to a new family or a new parent.

* I will be grateful, like Mary, for the blessings in my life and make it a point each day to praise God and rejoice with my family.

* I will share my time, treasure and talent with a pro-life or child advocacy program in my parish or community.

TWO

A Home Is Open to All
(Luke 2:1–7)

In those days a decree went out from Emperor Augustus that all the world should be registered. This was the first registration and was taken while Quirinius was governor of Syria. All went to their own towns to be registered. Joseph also went from the town of Nazareth in Galilee to Judea, to the city of David called Bethlehem, because he was descended from the house and family of David. He went to be registered with Mary, to whom he was engaged and who was expecting a child. While they were there, the time came for her to deliver her child. And she gave birth to her firstborn son and wrapped him in bands of cloth, and laid him in a manger, because there was no place for them in the inn.

OF ALL THE STORIES IN THE GOSPELS I BELIEVE THAT THIS IS THE MOST MIS-understood in regards to the home. Countless songs, plays and traditions have crept into our consciousness over the years concerning this story dating back as far as the non-canonical Gospel of James written in the year AD 200. The images of a late night birth, a grumpy innkeeper and a pregnant Mary and Joseph being put out of the house due to lack of room is not in the text. The traditions we have laid upon this story and our Western misunderstanding of Middle Eastern homes do a grave injustice to the people of the Middle East whose hospitality is legendary. The very idea that Jesus was born outside the home because there was no room for him is nothing less than preposterous and unimaginable! To think that a family member of the "house and family of David" would be denied lodging in a relative's home of the town of his birth not only goes against common sense but reveals a poor translation of the Greek word that translates as "inn."

Our Christmas memories and traditions surrounding this text may be a little imperfect, but hopefully the truth of the text will come out and provide deeper insight into the Word of God and allow us to bring forth new traditions. The word "inn" appears twice in the Gospel of Luke, once in this story and once in the parable of the Good Samaritan (Luke 10:25–37), where the Samaritan takes the wounded man to an inn. There are two different Greek words for inn used in Luke. *Pandocheion*, used in the Good Samaritan story, describes a place of lodging. It could be a humble place to lay down on the ground for the night or a public building where money was charged for lodging. The word here in the birth story is *kataluma*, which is a guest room in a house. (This is also the same word Matthew uses for the place that the disciples gathered for the Last Supper.)

With this information we can see how it would have been perfectly acceptable to have the child born in a home. There was no room in the guest room of the house, perhaps because other relatives were present for the census, so it is plausible that Jesus was born in the main living area and wrapped in swaddling clothes and placed in the manger inside the home.

Then what about the manger? Every feeding trough for animals I've ever seen has been outside of the house! This may be true in the West but not so in the Middle East. Animals' mangers were inside of the home. In 1 Samuel 28:24 the woman of Endor untied her calf "in the house," which she brought outside and slaughtered. Jesus himself makes reference to untying animals in the house when he cures a woman who had been crippled for eighteen years (Luke 13:10–17). Most people in Jesus' day had their animals with them in the house each evening, when they could provide warmth, and in the morning they untied them and led them outside.

The home that Jesus was born in was crowded, but the owners of the house made room for all of them. I wonder what people made of Joseph traveling with his pregnant wife as they ascended toward Bethlehem, for her presence was not needed for the census; this was the business of men. If Joseph had not taken Mary with him, she may have been exposed to the law and possibly stoned to death in Nazareth. Joseph, silent as he is, showed protective love toward Mary and his unborn son. The family of Joseph welcomed them into their home and what a difference the welcome made.

Artwork depicting the manger scene rarely, if ever, shows people other than Mary present, but this couldn't have been the way it was; others must have been present. Although many things have changed since the time of Jesus' birth, one thing hasn't— that is the drawing power of babies!

Babies have the awesome ability to draw attention unto themselves. My sister-in-law's newborn baby boy, John Paul, had

+ + +

"THE FAMILY IS THE FIRST SETTING OF EVANGELIZATION, THE PLACE WHERE THE GOOD NEWS OF CHRIST IS FIRST RECEIVED AND THEN, IN SIMPLE YET PROFOUND WAYS, HANDED ON FROM GENERATION TO GENERATION."

—Pope John Paul II, Meeting with African Americans, New Orleans, 1987[3] drawn people from four states in a matter of days. He was surrounded by Nanas, Grampys, a sister and brothers, cousins and friends and neighbors. Would the small village community of Bethlehem have been much different? One can witness in small villages today in developing countries how the community takes care of and provides for the newborn and mother. Certainly, this image of Mary in the barn alone is more a creation of our own imaginations than the biblical and historical situation.

I wonder if our lives today are busier or less hectic than those of Joseph and Mary. Everyone I know is stretched to the limit with work and family obligations, and if you have children forget about it! Much of my hectic schedule is my own fault and a result of filling in my calendar with too many commitments. This being said, do I take the time to prioritize those things in life that really are important? Is there room for Jesus in my home? Should any room in my house or area of my life be so filled and occupied that there is no room for him? Do I, like the owners of the home Jesus was born in, need to do some rearranging from time to time to make sure Jesus is a priority and that I have room for him? When we allow Jesus in, we are changed, but not us alone, our families too. We become more Christ-like and that changes the dynamic of the family and whatever environment we find ourselves in.

The room in which a newborn is placed becomes the room of prominence. Careful attention is placed to the child's every movement and need. Listening devices are set up to detect the child's slightest whimper, feeding schedules are tightly monitored and diapers are stocked to make sure nothing runs out. As time goes by, however, the monitoring decreases and the comfort level of the parents increases.

In our commitment to Christ there can be a danger of not paying attention to our spiritual life as time goes by. The newness of our faith can become routine. That groove we were in can become a rut. We would never allow this to happen with our children, but do we allow this to happen with our faith? It is normal for our faith experience to change and develop over time but, like a child, we must always nurture it and allow it to grow. Each new stage of life allows us opportunities to grow.

The manger is a place of nourishment. Luke mentions on three separate occasions that Jesus was placed there by Mary. I think this is a sign to us to look to "Jesus our hope" for our nourishment and sustenance. It can be difficult to do in our busy lives, but if we're too busy for God then we're simply just too busy. I think there are a number of ways to make the presence of Jesus known in the home by sign, symbol and action. Whatever you're inspired to do to make Christ known in the home, invite the input of others who live with you. Giving our family members ownership in the process will in itself be a good start.

Joseph and Mary were welcomed in this house, as well as the shepherds, Magi and others who came to visit. I'm sure they were never the same. Because of their hospitality Jesus was born in a home, humble as it may have been. That home continues to be a sign for you and me that we should open our doors to Christ and to all who are in need. We are welcome around the manger because he came for the likes of us.

PRAYER

Jesus, Mary and Joseph, you experienced the hospitality of family and so Jesus was born in a simple home. Make our homes a place where you are welcomed, loved and adored. May those who enter our own homes experience the loving presence of Jesus in word and action and may your presence light up our homes with the light of Christ. Keep close to your Sacred Heart all those who are shut out of their homes due to unplanned pregnancy or turmoil within the family. May the poor and rich alike find Christ in whatever state of life they are in and may they remember always to open wide the doors of their heart to Christ. Protect the most vulnerable among us, especially those who have lost their home due to natural disasters. Move in the hearts of Christians to respond to them as they would to Jesus himself. We ask this in Jesus' name. Amen.

REFLECTION QUESTIONS

1. What is your earliest or favorite Christmas memory?
2. Do you have any favorite Christmas songs or traditions that you celebrate as a family?
3. The infant Jesus certainly made his presence known both near and far. How does Christ make himself most present to you in your life?
4. What "nourishes" and "sustains" your faith? Has it changed over the years?

CHAPTER CHALLENGES

- I will make sure that Jesus is present in my home through symbol and hospitality.
- I will celebrate Christmas more expectantly by participating in Advent activities with the parish and in my home.
- I will support organizations that protect women, families and the unborn child with my time, treasure and talent.

THREE

A Home Is Where They Found Christ

(Matthew 2:9–12)

Birth.

When they had heard the king, they set out; and there, ahead of them, went the star that they had seen at its rising, until it stopped over the place where the child was. When they saw that the star had stopped, they were overwhelmed with joy. On entering the house, they saw the child with Mary his mother; and they knelt down and paid him homage. Then, opening their treasure chests, they offered him gifts of gold, frankincense, and myrrh. And having been warned in a dream not to return to Herod, they left for their own country by another road.

THE STORY OF THE WISE MEN IS TOLD OVER AND OVER AGAIN EACH Christmas. Every new generation hears of their remarkable journey from the East, encountering King Herod and setting out find the Messiah, led only by the star that set over the place where they were to stop. "O little town of Bethlehem...." The story has been memorialized in songs and paintings and in elementary school Christmas plays through the years. It is these unnamed, gentile,

"wise men" who give the child Jesus the title, "King of the Jews."
It is a title that will be used to taunt Jesus at his death, but first we
focus on Matthew's Gospel, where we are told that the wise men
"entered the house." They found Christ at home.

Combining the birth stories of Luke and Matthew, we have
acquired images throughout the ages of Jesus being rejected at
homes in Bethlehem and the Holy Family taking refuge in a barn.
This shows a misunderstanding of Middle Eastern hospitality and
the way homes were designed in the Middle East. It reveals more
of our ideas of homes in more modern and Western cultures. It is
totally unimaginable that a pregnant woman would be turned
away from the home while about to give birth. Would you turn
away a pregnant family member about to give birth, if she came
knocking on your door? Certainly not! In the Middle East, where
the whole society is guided by the values of honor and shame,
turning away a pregnant woman would have been inconceivable
and beyond belief. The construction of first-century Middle
Eastern homes had a living room with a few steps rising to it,
which contained an elevated sleeping area for the family. It was
common for families to have a manger, a feeding trough, for the
animals in the home. The animals would come into the house in
the evening and a manger was the place of feeding. It is most
likely that in the home, as both Matthew and a correct understanding of Luke's Gospel attest, that Jesus was born.

What an extraordinary scene it must have been to see these
strangely dressed and foreign visitors enter this humble home
and offer gifts to Jesus. Any person who has ever visited a newborn in the home knows that there is also a *new mother* in the
house as well, for the mother and child are inseparable. The bond
between newborn and mother is difficult to put into words. One
can objectively observe and try to describe the relationship, but
words fail to give justice to the protective love and care of a new

mother. One can only look at the woman and child and smile in joy. Such was the case I'm sure when the wise men entered the house. They witnessed the care and love of a new mother holding the child intimately in her arms.

They found Christ in the home.

The position of these wise men is admirable; they kneel and worship Jesus in the company of Mary and offer their gifts. When thinking about these gifts, I wonder if they were wrapped like so many of our gifts are. They probably didn't have fancy paper and ribbons and bows, but I imagine they were somehow wrapped, perhaps in a simple cloth with a string to hold it together. I wonder how the gifts were unwrapped. I can think back to my years as a child, and as an adult, when I tended to ignore the care in wrapping and tore apart the packaging to get to the gift. Paper is flying and ribbon is stretched to its breaking point all in order to go after what's inside. In reading this story it's easy to get sidetracked into thinking that the gifts are gold, frankincense and myrrh. The real gift is Jesus.

How do we "unwrap," so to speak, the gift of Jesus in our lives? He is presented to us as a child each Christmas. We prepare for the gift each Advent, yet do we have difficulty receiving him afterward? I believe people often don't know what to do with him. Like a strange gift from Aunt Amber or crazy Uncle Jordan, Jesus is a gift that we need to unwrap. On the other hand, do we believe we already *know* the gift? Have we adopted the attitude of, "OK, I understand. I get it. Jesus is born. I've heard this story

✚ ✚ ✚

"HELP PEOPLE TO DIS-COVER THE TRUE STAR WHICH POINTS OUT THE WAY TO US: JESUS CHRIST! LET US SEEK TO KNOW HIM BETTER AND BETTER, SO AS TO BE ABLE TO GUIDE OTHERS TO HIM WITH CONVICTION.

—Pope Benedict XVI, World Youth Day Homily, August 21, 2005[4]

before, I know how it will end." Somehow there is a temptation to think that Jesus is a re-gift! In a sense he is! But I would not say that he is the same old Jesus because, while he may not change, we do. Jesus desires to come to us as we are during each year and stage of our lives. He desires to enter into our lives and to refresh us anew with his love.

Most likely the process of unwrapping is a slow one; we are not designed to receive him all at once, for it would be too much. As we grow older, some gifts lose their appeal or we just grow out of them. Not so with Jesus. He is a gift we grow into, gradually allowing him to reveal his love to us anew each day as we grow and change and move on through the different phases of our lives. Unwrapping the gift can be exciting with anticipation of *what's next?* At times the gift may seem strange until we understand how he works and moves and we adjust ourselves to him. Like most children with presents, we long for more. Jesus doesn't fail to satisfy. At each new moment in our lives he is waiting to reveal himself to us in new and familiar ways, hoping that we don't disregard the gift that is himself.

Where do you find the presence of Christ? Have you considered looking in your home? I'm sure we can catch a glimpse of his presence with eyes opened by the Holy Spirit. If Christ's presence is unrecognizable by you in your home, can you be the presence of Christ by your words and deeds? Will you, by your forgiveness, mercy and love, be the light to your home and family? That is the challenge of us all who have received the gift of Jesus with joy.

In our homes the gift is not what we have but who we are in Jesus. It's easy to get sidetracked by fancy homes with all the conveniences and ignore the people. The home the wise men entered was one where Christ was present. The *real presence* of Jesus was in the home and recognized by wise men and a humble mother. We would do well to recognize the presence of Jesus in our homes in the presence of family who are made in the image and likeness of God. May we recognize the special presence of Jesus in our family members and accept them with all the love and care of a mother.

We are told that the wise men left by another route and most likely *went home*. How were their lives different because of the presence of Jesus in the house? How will your life be different because of your encounter with him? May we, too, be wise men and women by seeking Christ and bringing the Good News into our homes.

PRAYER

Father in heaven, you are close to us; you are Emmanuel, God with us. Refresh us and renew us each day with your love. Remind us that each day is a gift to be unwrapped and that nothing comes to us except through your hands. Give us the strength, wisdom and perseverance of the wise men who sought you in lowly places, in the home. May we seek Christ in all whom we encounter. May our homes be filled by the presence of Jesus in our actions and in our words. Grant us the joy of opening up our gifts and talents before you to a world which needs your presence. We ask this through Christ our Lord. Amen.

REFLECTION QUESTIONS

1. What is your favorite childhood memory of Christmas?
2. Were there any outward signs of Jesus' presence in your home growing up?
3. How has your early home life formed your faith?
4. What was your first encounter with Jesus? What stands out as you recall how you were introduced to him?
5. How do you receive the gift of God in Jesus?
6. How can you be a "present" to another like Jesus is?

CHAPTER CHALLENGES

- We will write down an inventory of our family's gifts and talents, and as a family we will be intentional in donating a portion of them to an organization where we can best use these gifts and talents.
- I will take some time each day to quietly meditate on the life of Jesus and be attentive to the Spirit as were the wise men.
- I will gather my family and together we will pray and commit ourselves as a family to a specific *need* during the different liturgical seasons.

FOUR

A Home Is Where We Find Our Father

(Luke 2:48–52)

When his parents saw him they were astonished; and his mother said to him, "Child, why have you treated us like this? Look, your father and I have been searching for you in great anxiety." *He said to them, "Why were you searching for me? Did you not know that I must be in my Father's house?"* But they did not understand what he said to them. Then he went down with them and came to Nazareth, and was obedient to them. His mother treasured all these things in her heart.

And Jesus increased in wisdom and in years, and in divine and human favor.

MARY AND JOSEPH FOUND JESUS IN A PLACE OF WORSHIP AFTER THREE days of searching. It can be said that Jesus confused, frightened and even questioned his parents in this short passage from his early life found only in Luke's Gospel, but he did not dishonor them. This insight into the hidden years of Jesus was certainly a cause for alarm for his parents. Most parents experience, sometimes daily, the bewildering actions of their children that sometimes can even be quite embarrassing. In this glimpse into the life of the child Jesus in the temple, we, too, get an indication of Jesus' self-understanding and his relationship with his Father.

While we don't know when Joseph died, we know by this passage that he was still alive when Jesus was twelve years old, and we can reasonably assume that Joseph was a wonderful father to Jesus, for there is nothing in Scripture or tradition to suggest otherwise. When Jesus speaks of earthly fathers in the Scriptures, the term is always used tenderly, in the best sense of what fathers are. Recall Jesus' words when he said, "Is there anyone among you who, if your child asks for bread, will give a stone? Or if the child asks for a fish, will give a snake?" (Matthew 7:9–10). Bear in mind as well, that the image of God in the Prodigal Son is one of a seeking father, one who undergoes humiliation in order to protect his son. The tender image of a father who loves like a mother was in part most likely modeled in the home by Joseph, faithful husband, loving father.

In this story we hear Jesus speaking about his "Father's house." Regardless of how one interprets these words, they can certainly seem harsh and insensitive if one is listening with the ears of Joseph. It may seem to us that Jesus' parents were hurt by these statements, Joseph particularly. Although what Jesus said may have caused some hurt or at least confusion in the hearts of Joseph and Mary, his words do not reveal a rejection of his parents. Rather, they reveal a new understanding of himself in relation to God, an unfolding relationship in which Jesus understands that the temple is his "Father's house."

As a teacher I've enjoyed many reunions with my former students. It makes little difference if the reunion takes place a year later or ten years later, at a diner, through e-mail or at a formal

✛ ✛ ✛

"THIS BOND OF CHARITY WAS THE CORE OF THE HOLY
FAMILY'S LIFE, FIRST IN THE POVERTY OF BETHLEHEM,
THEN IN THEIR EXILE IN EGYPT, AND LATER IN THE HOUSE
OF NAZARETH. THE CHURCH DEEPLY VENERATES THIS
FAMILY, AND PROPOSES IT AS THE MODEL OF ALL FAMILIES.
INSERTED DIRECTLY IN THE MYSTERY OF THE
INCARNATION, THE FAMILY OF NAZARETH HAS ITS OWN
SPECIAL MYSTERY. AND IN THIS MYSTERY, AS IN THE
INCARNATION, ONE FINDS A TRUE FATHERHOOD: THE
HUMAN FORM OF THE FAMILY OF THE SON OF GOD, A TRUE
HUMAN FAMILY FORMED BY THE DIVINE MYSTERY. IN THIS
FAMILY, JOSEPH IS THE FATHER: HIS FATHERHOOD IS NOT
ONE THAT DERIVES FROM BEGETTING OFFSPRING; BUT NEI-
THER IS IT AN 'APPARENT' OR MERELY 'SUBSTITUTE'
FATHERHOOD. RATHER, IT IS ONE THAT FULLY SHARES IN
AUTHENTIC HUMAN FATHERHOOD AND THE MISSION OF A
FATHER IN THE FAMILY. THIS IS A CONSEQUENCE OF THE
HYPOSTATIC UNION: HUMANITY TAKEN UP INTO THE UNITY
OF THE DIVINE PERSON OF THE WORD-SON, JESUS CHRIST.
TOGETHER WITH HUMAN NATURE, ALL THAT IS HUMAN, AND
ESPECIALLY THE FAMILY—AS THE FIRST DIMENSION OF
MAN'S EXISTENCE IN THE WORLD—IS ALSO TAKEN UP IN
CHRIST. WITHIN THIS CONTEXT, JOSEPH'S HUMAN FATHER-
HOOD WAS ALSO 'TAKEN UP' IN THE MYSTERY OF CHRIST'S
INCARNATION."

—John Paul II, *Redemptoris Custos*[5]

reunion; it is always a memorable time. One of the things I enjoy
about reconnecting with my former students is listening to their
stories and learning about what brought them to their current
career or situation. Some students take me for a loop when I find

out what they're doing, and I had never imagined the student taking this direction in life. For most, however, I can say there was a hint or a foreshadowing of their calling in high school. The students' empathy and compassion led them to a career as a nurse or counselor. Other student's abilities to lead and listen move them toward teaching. Perhaps in this story, Jesus is giving his parents a glimpse into the future and into his ministry that would change the world.

Just as our Blessed Mother cherished these moments in her heart, as Scripture tells us, so too do all parents treasure the small yet significant memories that their children make. Baby books and scrapbooks are popular ways of chronicling these benchmarks of life. They bring us back to those first moments. The first smile, the first real belly laugh, the first few steps and the first words are tucked away on those pages and in the heart. We follow the footsteps of the Blessed Mother who did just the same thing with her Child. I have no doubt that Joseph treasured these things in his heart as well. I have made it a point to write a letter to my daughter during each Christmas, Valentine's Day and on her birthday. Although she is barely three years old, it's a way for me to chronicle the important events in our lives and a way to express my love for her even before she can really respond.

Jesus, Mary and Joseph probably returned home as a family, reflecting on their experience in Jerusalem and what it may have meant for them in the future. It would appear that back in the home things returned to normal, for nothing is noted in Scripture that tells us otherwise.

The next momentous occasion we will learn about in Scripture is when Jesus enters the synagogue in Capernaum one particular sabbath, unrolls the scroll and begins his public ministry. Jesus continues to learn the family trade from Joseph and the study of the Torah, which prepares him for his mission. The home, most importantly, is where Jesus "increased in wisdom and in years, and in divine and human favor."

Of all the prestigious and expensive schools some students attend today, can any compare to the home of Joseph and Mary? That must have been a real school of love! Consider the lessons Joseph passed on to Jesus, not simply lessons dealing with the tools of the trade, but lessons about life and how to communicate with people, how to use words to persuade others and how business transactions work. The facial expressions and body language of Joseph when dealing with friends, oppressors and suspicious characters must have been noticed by Jesus. Jesus learned from the holy example set by Joseph.

By no means did Joseph serve as Jesus' sole teacher. Certainly he spent much of the day with Mary, his mother. Talk about a graduate school! Imagine the impact Mary had on the compassion of Jesus, the justice and mercy of Christ, the forgiveness that all came out and overflowed in the teaching and life of her son. No doubt his profound respect for women was modeled and lived out in the home and on the streets of Nazareth; true God and true man, formed in the heart of God from the beginning, one in being with the Father. Like us, Jesus was "schooled" in a home.

I'm sure that there are some people who believe that I'm reading too much into the influence of Jesus' early formation from his earthly parents. Jesus was, of course, divine. Yet perhaps we've allowed ourselves some distance from Christ by emphasizing his divinity and neglecting his humanity. While they are both united in Jesus, I think it can be a "both and" understanding, rather than emphasizing one and neglecting the other.

Jesus exclaimed in the temple that this is "my" Father's house, not "the" Father's house, or even "our" Father's house. His zeal and love for God had an intimate character to it that would lead him to turn over the tables of those selling goods in order to make a profit from his Father's house. When he taught his disciples to pray, however, he told us to call God "Our Father." The personal relationship he had with the Father was one that was about to be opened up to all who believe and thus unite us to God and each other, as it was in the beginning. It was, and is, an invitation for us to enter into this relationship with God the Father and each other, in a new and yet ancient way, unseen since the time of Adam.

God is still calling out to those who can hear his voice as he called out to Adam, "Where are you?" (Genesis 3:9). Christ calls us into his Father's house where he is present and gives himself to us out of love through Word and sacrament. He is still found in a place of worship, body, blood, soul and divinity in the Eucharist. His blood runs through our veins; we share in the one body; we are one family in God, our Father.

PRAYER

Loving Jesus, you were sent from the very heart of God the Father and were formed in the home of Mary and Joseph, a home of reverence and a school of love. Help us to make our homes places where you are honored through our sacrifices for one another. We pray for those who are fatherless on this earth; comfort them with the knowledge and love of God, our Father, and let them experience the Father's love in tangible ways. Watch over parents of missing children and protect children from being lost or separated from their parents. Fill our hearts and homes with the joy of being reconciled to you and each other until we meet you face to face in heaven. Saint Joseph, patron of fathers, pray for us. Amen.

REFLECTION QUESTIONS

1. Jesus is in the temple asking questions and listening. How do you put yourself in a position to listen to God or learn about your faith?

2. Who has influenced you in your faith life? Was it one person or a number of people who helped form you through the years?

3. What things do you think God treasures about you and writes down in his book?

4. What experiences have formed your faith in the home?

CHAPTER CHALLENGES

• I will actively seek to improve my relationship with God by being faithful in reading a portion of Scripture each day.

• I will make a visit with Jesus at a Catholic church or find a parish which has eucharistic adoration and spend time being with God.

• I will share my resources and collaborate with others in helping children become all God calls them to be.

FIVE

Jesus Made His Home in Nazareth
(Matthew 2:19–23)

When Herod died, an angel of the Lord suddenly appeared in a dream to Joseph in Egypt and said, "Get up, take the child and his mother, and go to the land of Israel, for those who were seeking the child's life are dead." Then Joseph got up, took the child and his mother, and went to the land of Israel. But when he heard that Archelaus was ruling over Judea in place of his father Herod, he was afraid to go there. And after being warned in a dream, he went away to the district of Galilee. *There he made his home in a town called Nazareth, so that what had been spoken through the prophets might be fulfilled, "He will be called a Nazorean."*

TODAY WE CALL JESUS BY MANY NAMES: MESSIAH, LORD, GOOD Shepherd, Emmanuel, the Bread of Life, Teacher, as well as many other titles found in the New Testament. Rarely, if ever, do we refer to Jesus as a Nazorean. I'm convinced that if today I mentioned to my friends that I was giving a talk about "the Nazorean" they would have little idea of whom I was speaking. Yet this is the title Jesus will be known by early on in his life.

We are told that Joseph listened to the angel and headed back to Israel with his wife and child as the angel directed him to do. Israel, however, is a big country for one traveling on foot and decisions have to be made about *where* in Israel to stay. Joseph, again attentive and obedient to the warning in the dream, changed plans and made his home in Nazareth. Joseph, we are told, was afraid, not for his life but for that of the family, hence, the change of plans. It seems Joseph was attentive to the political climate of the day as well as where work could be found, which is essential in raising a family and providing for them. Although Joseph is silent in the Scriptures, his actions speak for him, actions of a caring father attentive to the Spirit and willing to change course for the protection of his family.

Archaeologists tell us that Nazareth was a prime location due to its proximity to Sepphoris, a town that Herod Antipas was rebuilding as his capital. Building was certainly an important trade that could support Joseph's family, and this trade he would pass on to Jesus. Some scholars suggest that Jesus and Joseph would never have worked for Herod Antipas

✛ ✛ ✛

"THE FINDING OF JESUS IN THE TEMPLE IS THE ONLY EVENT THAT BREAKS THE SILENCE OF THE GOSPELS ABOUT THE HIDDEN YEARS OF JESUS (CF. LK 2:41-52). HERE JESUS LETS US CATCH A GLIMPSE OF THE MYSTERY OF HIS TOTAL CONSECRATION TO A MISSION THAT FLOWS FROM HIS DIVINE SONSHIP: 'DID YOU NOT KNOW THAT I MUST BE ABOUT MY FATHER'S WORK?' (LK 2:49 ALT). MARY AND JOSEPH DID NOT UNDERSTAND THESE WORDS, BUT THEY ACCEPTED THEM IN FAITH. MARY 'KEPT ALL THESE THINGS IN HER HEART' DURING THE YEARS JESUS REMAINED HIDDEN IN THE SILENCE OF AN ORDINARY LIFE."
—*Catechism of the Catholic Church*, 534[6]

or any of his building projects because the city of Sepphoris had theaters, stadiums, graven images and other projects that went against Jewish law and custom. I can imagine, however, be it in Sepphoris or Nazareth, Jesus and Joseph walking together early in the morning to work, then working on the building projects— tools hanging by their sides—while Mary, back at home, prepared a hearty meal for them.

I wonder what the home of the Holy Family actually looked and *felt* like. I'm sure archaeologists can give us insight into the physical structure of a first-century Nazorean home, but I wonder what the atmosphere was like inside. Everyone experiences homes that are warm, welcoming and hospitable, with décor and furnishings on the outside that speak of a welcoming place. On the other hand, there are homes which seem cold, uninviting and inhospitable. The differences between the two have a little to do with the size or structure of the house but most of all with the warmth of the people inside and their love. In a culture where hospitality is legendary, I can imagine a very welcoming home even if the furnishings were meager by today's standards.

This is the beginning of what scholars call the "hidden years" of Jesus. We hear of Jesus being lost in the temple in Luke's Gospel as a young man, but aside from that story we know very little of what happened to Jesus...or do we? I think there is some- thing to be said for the parenting skills of Mary and Joseph that reveal what Jesus experienced through these "hidden years" in the home.

As a high school teacher for many years I can tell a great deal about a young person's home from how they present themselves to the world. I'm never one hundred percent accurate, but I can get a very good sense of what has gone on in the home after observing the students and hearing their stories, reading their homework assignments, listening to their prayers and very often by the expressions on their faces. Their self-esteem, enthusiasm for life, cheerfulness and willingness to pray and stand up for their beliefs speak a great deal about how they were raised. They have come from a home where love and sacrifice is the norm, never a perfect home, but a healthy home. When meeting the parents of these students, I try to make a point of complimenting them on doing a wonderful job. On the other hand, when watching stories on TV about people who have committed heinous crimes, I usually see the defense begin by describing a horrific home life, one marked by neglect and abuse. Father Thomas A. Judge, founder of four religious orders, was right when he said, "Save the child and you save all."

Although this passage by Matthew about Jesus making his home in Nazareth does not give a lot of detail, I believe we can gather some insights by how Jesus relates to people and uses everyday household objects and imagery in his preaching. Jesus was born of a woman into a family and so experienced and grasped all that being a family member entailed. This fact was reflected in how Jesus spread his message and in how he related to people.

Consider some of the images Jesus uses in his teaching: a woman lighting a lamp and placing it on a lamp stand, a woman kneading yeast into dough, straining wine for insects, a friend arriving at midnight, a family dispute and a wayward son that leads to a divided family, a house built on rock, an appreciation for the birds of the air and the flowers in the field and a man giving a great banquet. All of these stories and images can relate to family and life at home. Jesus must have experienced a wonderful home life with the love and care of Mary and Joseph and his extended family. One thing learned by living in a small village like Nazareth is that one relies on and needs others to survive. This is an idea that we would do well to implement and teach our children.

Perhaps in reflecting on that home in Nazareth, the home that formed Jesus, we can reflect on our own homes and the lessons in life and in faith that were taught by words and caught by example. In doing so, maybe we can model family life as it's meant to be.

PRAYER

Jesus, Lord of heaven and earth, you made your home in the obscure village of Nazareth with Mary and Joseph by your side watching over and protecting you. We thank you for the gift of family and for the confidence that you are with us, watching over us as your children. Watch over the homes in which we live, raise children and share meals and the sorrows and joys of life. Grant parents the wisdom and love of Saints Joseph and Mary that will enable them to raise healthy children who love God, neighbor and themselves. We pray for the homeless, who do not share in the gift of shelter. Use our gifts and talents to provide for their needs, for when we help them we are giving direct aid to you. We pray this in Jesus' name and in the power of the Holy Spirit. Amen.

REFLECTION QUESTIONS

1. What did the home of Jesus, Mary and Joseph look and feel like? Can you imagine yourself as a guest in their home? What would you experience as you were welcomed in?
2. Are there any places besides the home you grew up in that you would consider home? Why? What qualities do these places have?
3. If Jesus were to knock on your door, would you be reluctant to let him in your house? Would he feel welcome or would it be uncomfortable for you?
4. Are there any "rooms" in your life, so to speak, that you would

need to tidy up before Jesus was allowed in? Are there a couple of closets or unrepented sins or jealousies that you want him to help "clean up"?

CHAPTER CHALLENGES

- I will pray for and find a way to help support those who are victims of natural disasters and those who are homeless.
- I will volunteer my time to help educate new parents or single parents with the skills they need to raise a family and to manage their resources.
- I will have a specific *family time* each day to talk, share faith and laugh with the other members of my family.

SIX

A Home Experiences the Healing Touch of Jesus
(Mark 1:29–35)

As soon as they left the synagogue, they entered the house of Simon and Andrew, with James and John. Now Simon's mother-in-law was in bed with a fever, and they told him about her at once. He came and took her by the hand and lifted her up. Then the fever left her, and she began to serve them.

That evening, at sunset, they brought to him all who were sick or possessed with demons. And the whole city was gathered around the door. And he cured many who were sick with various diseases, and cast out many demons; and he would not permit the demons to speak, because they knew him.

In the morning, while it was still very dark, he got up and went out to a deserted place, and there he prayed.

AFTER THE DISCIPLES LEAVE THE HOUSE OF GOD, GOD ENTERS THE HOUSE of the disciples. The movement of the disciples from the synagogue to a home is the movement of the early Christian community. As Christians were expelled from the synagogue, they gathered in the homes of believers to devote themselves to the

44

teaching of the apostles, fellowship, the breaking of bread and prayers. This miracle story about an unnamed woman with a common fever seems relatively insignificant. Many miracles are steeped in the tradition of the Hebrew Scriptures and have extensive theology underlying them. Take for instance the miracle of the loaves and fish or when Jesus opened the eyes of the blind; these and many more miracles point to an even greater reality and sign for the people. This miracle seems small in comparison; although I'm sure the woman who was healed might disagree. Nonetheless, it seems that the Christian community thought it was significant because it is included in three of the Gospels.

I've found it remarkable that neither Jesus nor the sick woman say a word. In addition to their silence, it is striking that the miracle takes place in the home, a home much like yours and mine. A home where a sickness occurs that affects a member of the house so that business is not as usual, where other members have to make up for what is lacking. This sickness affected not just the mother-in-law but the whole family.

✢ ✢ ✢

"THE LAITY, BY THEIR VERY VOCATION, SEEK THE KINGDOM OF GOD BY ENGAGING IN TEM- PORAL AFFAIRS AND BY ORDERING THEM ACCORDING TO THE PLAN OF GOD. THEY LIVE IN THE WORLD, THAT IS, IN EACH AND IN ALL OF THE SECU- LAR PROFESSIONS AND OCCUPATIONS. THEY LIVE IN THE ORDINARY CIRCUMSTANCES OF FAMILY AND SOCIAL LIFE, FROM WHICH THE VERY WEB OF THEIR EXISTENCE IS WOVEN. THEY ARE CALLED THERE BY GOD THAT BY EXERCISING THEIR PROPER FUNC- TION AND LED BY THE SPIRIT OF THE GOSPEL THEY MAY WORK FOR THE SANCTIFICATION OF THE WORLD FROM WITHIN AS A LEAVEN."

—Dogmatic Constitution on the Church, 31[7]

Isn't that true in our families as well? When one person suffers, the entire family and community suffer. We are concerned for the welfare of the person and her family. I'm not only talking about the nuclear family but other extended families that touch our lives such as coworkers, friends, teammates, classmates or fellow parishioners. When we find out someone is in trouble, it compels us to pray, to reach out with a card, letter or meal. Illness, be it depression, addiction, physical trauma or just the flu, takes its toll on a family.

Such is the case in these few verses of Mark's Gospel. The disciples were not afraid to invite Jesus into a house that was experiencing illness. Jesus, likewise, was not afraid to enter. He walked right in. I wonder what would have happened if the disciples had said, "Let's not invite Jesus over until everything is perfect and everyone is healthy"? If that were the case, would we ever feel comfortable enough to invite in Jesus? Most likely we wouldn't. We are always in some sort of turmoil or anxiety or stress, or at least for most people things are never one hundred percent normal. We could always use a few more hours in the day or at least a few more minutes to get ready for the next event. Jesus desires to come in anyway, even when we are a mess. He desires to comfort and heal the illness and brokenness that we experience and that affects the whole family. Heal a person, heal a family.

What a difference that healing must have had on the family. Her parents could sleep a little better knowing that their daughter was OK and that this fever wasn't the beginning of a serious illness. Saint Peter could relax knowing that his mother-in-law was healed and that he could get back to a full work schedule. The family, which included everyone in the village, no longer had to work a little harder to provide the bread and water she could not. The family was restored to its working order by the touch of Jesus.

The woman responded with service and what a beautiful response that was.

This story of Jesus entering the house that experienced sickness didn't end there. We are told that in the evening, when the sabbath had ended, the whole city gathered around her door. What a difference the healing presence of Jesus made that day. Not one family but an entire community was affected and came to experience the healing touch of Christ.

Our homes need the healing presence of Christ today as well. Not that all of our families are dysfunctional or racked with illness but like this home that Jesus entered, our homes need the touch of Christ. Our families need the touch of Christ. Whatever the sickness, a Christian home invites Jesus in and allows him to work through the Spirit and through each one of us.

The families that we come into contact with may not always be as bold as those first disciples. Unfortunately, illnesses in many homes are covered up due to shame and embarrassment. Even pride may prevent some from asking for the help of others when there is sickness, believing falsely that we are designed to handle all of our problems alone. In these cases we may need to be sensitive and creative in recognizing the illness and in offering help. We can't and shouldn't force our help on anyone, but we should be available to others, which certainly may be a start to opening doors.

What will your story be? We live it out like Jesus and these disciples every time we enter a home. May our presence bring healing and peace to those whose homes we enter.

PRAYER

God of mercy and love, we see that you willingly accepted the invitation to enter a home that experienced illness. Enter into our homes with your power to heal the brokenness that we experience no matter the illness, physical or mental, large or small. Come as our welcome guest. Forgive us for the times we were insensitive to the needs of others in our home and community and failed to extend a loving touch. Give us your vision to see illness even the small illnesses in life. Lend us your ears to hear to the sickness of mind and body. Jesus, as we have received from you, let us extend our healing touch to a world that desperately needs your healing presence so that we may continue your work on earth. We ask this in your precious name. Amen.

REFLECTION QUESTIONS

1. Can you remember a time when there was an illness in your family? How did it affect the family as a whole?
2. Have you ever reached out to a person in the community who was suffering? How did it make you feel? Was there any hesitation or reluctance on your part?
3. Have you ever withheld information about a particular hurt or illness because you felt it was too insignificant? Have you ever withheld it from God? Why?
4. Have you ever been touched in a positive way just by someone's actions? What was your response?
5. Have you ever experienced the comfort of a person reaching out to your family member? Did that act of kindness relieve some anxiety or stress on your part?

CHAPTER CHALLENGES

• I will be more sensitive to those around me who experience illness and offer to assist them in some significant way, be it ever so small.
• I will prepare a meal or offer to go shopping for a family who has experienced an illness in the family or some sort of setback.
• I will set up a "prayer bowl" in my home under a cross or icon and place the names of people for whom our family is praying.

SEVEN

The Home Is a Place of Forgiveness and Healing
(Mark 2:1-12)

When he returned to Capernaum after some days, it was reported that he was at home. So many gathered around that there was no longer room for them, not even in front of the door; and he was speaking the word to them. Then some people came, bringing to him a paralyzed man, carried by four of them. And when they could not bring him to Jesus because of the crowd, they removed the roof above him; and after having dug through it, they let down the mat on which the paralytic lay. When Jesus saw their faith, he said to the paralytic, "Son, your sins are forgiven." Now some of the scribes were sitting there, questioning in their hearts, "Why does this fellow speak in this way? It is blasphemy! Who can forgive sins but God alone?" At once Jesus perceived in his spirit that they were discussing these questions among themselves; and he said to them, "Why do you raise such questions in your hearts? Which is easier, to say to the paralytic, 'Your sins are forgiven,' or to say, 'Stand up and take your mat and walk'? But so that you may know that the Son of Man has authority on earth to forgive sins"—he said to the paralytic—"*I say to you, stand up, take your mat and go to your home.*" And he stood up, and immediately took the mat and went out before all of them; so that they were all amazed and glorified God, saying, "We have never seen anything like this!"

"WE HAVE NEVER SEEN ANYTHING LIKE THIS!" THIS IS WHERE THE TEXT ends, but it is certainly not where the story ends. For what happened next is just as touching and heartwarming as what Jesus did inside the home. Can you imagine the walk back to the once-paralyzed man's home and family? In the same way I can vividly visualize four men carrying their friend on a mat toward the house where Jesus was present, I can equally envision the five friends walking arm in arm back home. I'm sure the restored and forgiven man stumbled a bit at first as he took his first few steps, relying on the support of his friends, but he soon got the hang of it. Did a crowd begin to follow them as he approached his home, curious at the reception he would receive? I think I would have followed at a little distance to see the reaction of this man's family and friends. Perhaps when they were about twenty or so paces from the front door the five men stopped and the four friends looked at their friend, now free from his paralysis and said, "This is it, go on and knock on the door yourself." I can picture his apprehension, and excitement as well, as he approaches. Immediately before he knocks, he looks back and gives his friends a smile. I imagine him gently knocking on the door and then taking a step back. On the other side I hear the shuffling of feet and then as the door opens wide, his mother stands there in awe, speechless. He steps forward, puts his arms around his mother and squeezes her tight for perhaps the first time in years. After a lengthy embrace he looks to his left and sees his wife stooping over the well, drawing up water. He quietly approaches, taps her on the shoulder. She turns and stands, wipes her hands

THE HOME IS A PLACE OF FORGIVENESS AND HEALING

on her apron in one fluid motion as she stands toe-to-toe with the man she married. In utter disbelief she embraces him, he whispers in her ear, "Thank you, honey, for standing by me all these years." Tears roll down both their cheeks as the words, "Daddy, Daddy," echo across the courtyard and his children grab hold of his legs and squeeze him with all their might. The crowd witnessing this breaks out in spontaneous applause and tears flow freely from everyone gathered.

On this day Jesus would be speaking the Word to a crowd that had gathered, a crowd that was more likely interested in the speaker of the Word

✠ ✠ ✠

"SO, I THINK THIS IS ESSENTIAL—FIND THE LORD, FIND THE SAINTS OF THE TIMES, BUT ALSO FIND THE NOT CANONIZED, SIMPLE PERSONS WHO ARE REALLY IN THE HEART OF THE CHURCH."

—Cardinal Joseph Ratzinger (Pope Benedict XVI), interview, September 5, 2003[8]

than the Word itself, although they were one and the same. The home this miracle was performed in witnessed faith, hope, love, forgiveness, healing and amazement, as well as questioning and doubt. The homes that the people went back to were most likely changed forever.

I am intrigued by the phrase, "it was reported that he was at home." Who reported this and why? Jesus had lived in Capernaum for some time and was probably known as the "carpenter" or "craftsman." What made his arrival home this time so important? Why were people rushing to get to the house? Why all the excitement at his arrival home? When examining Mark 1, we see Jesus at the very beginning of his ministry and he is recorded as doing some miraculous things. People wanted to see for themselves what had happened and if this was true. Where did Jesus begin preaching the Word in the city of Capernaum? At home!

The simplicity of Jesus' plan is something to take note of today. Often in our fast-paced society, bursting with instant communication and chaotic activity, we try to get our message out; we want to have our voice heard and get above "the buzz." Jesus might have begun his proclamation of the Good News in Jerusalem. After all, Satan himself took Jesus up to the pinnacle of the temple (archaeologists have found a stone that fell from the pinnacle of the temple after its fall in AD 70 upon which an inscription read, "The place of Trumpeting"). The pinnacle was the place where major announcements were made. Jesus may have considered starting in Rome; it was the center of the world by all accounts and his message could have received the attention of the wealthy, powerful and influential people of the time.

Jesus, however, was comfortable speaking the Word in the home. That was perhaps a reason people felt comfortable approaching him. I think of how some people may never enter the church because they have some level of discomfort or resentment against some particular church teaching or some emotional disconnect. If I expect to engage them, the church may not be the place. People will, however, meet in a home or a restaurant because they feel more comfortable; there's no baggage that sometimes accompanies a church building. I have at times had more opportunities to witness to my faith during a meal at home or a local diner than I've had in the church. Jesus takes the opportunity to speak to people where there is a level of comfort and familiarity, namely the home.

Jesus addresses the paralytic with the familial title of "Son." Not stranger, not sinner. Nor did he define him by his paralysis, but rather Jesus called him "Son." This man must have known that he was in the right house. In this house, in the midst of the crowd, he experiences the forgiveness and healing of Christ. The sin or sins we do not know, nor are they important, but the first words out of Jesus' mouth to him are words of forgiveness. Forgiveness is freely offered before any confession takes place. What a powerful example for us today to be forgiven in the home, forgiveness freely given, because we have been freely forgiven. Healing follows afterward.

I have to believe there is an intimate connection between forgiveness and healing. I do believe that what affects the spirit affects the body. When we are alienated from someone we love or suffering from guilt, it has an impact on us physiologically and our immune system is weakened. I remember once hearing from a grief counselor that when people enter a hospital for problems associated with ulcers or other stomach ailments there is almost always some trauma that occurred six months to a year before. The phrase, "confession is good for the soul" does seem to have some validity. The same goes for forgiveness.

The Gospel story concludes here but that's not where it ends. The story doesn't end with Jesus' command to stand and take up his mat. Jesus told him to "go home." We can only imagine what the man's life was like afterward. He probably spent every day onward telling the good news that affected him and his family. I can hear his wife or mother and father, after locating Jesus, saying, "Thank you. Thank you. Our son was dead and now is alive. Our family is restored after you forgave him and healed him." I can picture the restored man telling his grandchildren, "Did I ever tell you the time my friends brought me to Jesus...."

Thank God that most who are paralyzed today fare far better than those who suffered in antiquity. Understanding that a person is of value for who they are, rather than their physical condition or what they produce, can still be a challenge to those who marginalize the physically and mentally infirm or the elderly or those in the womb.

The experience of forgiveness and healing in a home—what a beautiful image and reality that we can make come alive today in our homes. Not much has changed in our homes, for being a member of a family will give us ample opportunities to practice these two virtues on a daily basis. Forgiveness and healing will test us at times to our breaking point as we, too, will challenge those around us. If you believe forgiving, healing and living like Jesus is easy, you've never tried it. Yet, these two qualities, forgiveness and healing, will mark us as followers of Christ. First start in the home and then move outward. You too will have people raising the roof in celebration.

PRAYER
Almighty God, your words continue to attract us to yourself as it did to those who gathered in the home so many years ago. Refresh us with your Word, provide us with a hunger and thirst for the Word of God. May it stir within us to draw us closer to you. Strengthen our faith so that it is persevering, unwavering, persistent and creative like those four friends of the paralyzed man. May our homes open up to your healing and forgiving presence. May all who enter experience your healing touch through us. We ask this through Christ our Lord, under the protection of the Holy Family. Amen.

REFLECTION QUESTIONS
1. Have you ever witnessed friends or yourself being creative and going the extra mile for a friend? What was the experience like?
2. Have you ever experienced forgiveness and healing in the home? How so?
3. Why do you think Jesus forgave the man before he healed him?
4. Jesus commands the man to go home. How were things different now that he was forgiven and healed?

5. Is there anyone in your family who needs forgiveness and healing? What can you do about it to help?

CHAPTER CHALLENGES

- I will think about becoming a eucharistic minister at my church or bringing the Eucharist to sick people in my parish.
- I will make an effort to recognize people who go quietly about their work and acknowledge them with a kind word or card.
- I will keep a prayer list and pray faithfully each day for the members of my family and others who are on it.

EIGHT

A Home Experiences a Taxing Meal

(Mark 2:13–17)

Jesus went out again beside the sea; the whole crowd gathered around him, and he taught them. As he was walking along, he saw Levi son of Alphaeus sitting at the tax booth, and he said to him, "Follow me." And he got up and followed him.

And as he sat at dinner in Levi's house, many tax collectors and sinners were also sitting with Jesus and his disciples—for there were many who followed him. When the scribes of the Pharisees saw that he was eating with sinners and tax collectors, they said to his disciples, "Why does he eat with tax collectors and sinners?" When Jesus heard this, he said to them, "Those who are well have no need of a physician, but those who are sick; I have come to call not the righteous but sinners."

FEW THINGS IN OUR SOCIETY BRING PEOPLE CLOSER TOGETHER THAN A meal; it has always been that way. Whether it's to celebrate a team victory, honor a retiree or to share an intimate occasion with a significant other, meals bring people close. Families, too, have the

✣   ✣   ✣

"DINNERTIME IN OUR HOUSEHOLD HAS ALWAYS BEEN
HECTIC. IT IS NOT OFTEN THAT WE SIT DOWN TOGETHER
AND EAT, BUT WHEN WE DO, IT IS ALWAYS NICE. I WILL
NEVER FORGET THE EASTER SUNDAY MEAL I SHARED WITH
MY ENTIRE FAMILY JUST AFTER HAVING ARRIVED HOME
FROM WORKING ABROAD FOR FOUR MONTHS. I DIDN'T
REALIZE HOW MUCH I MISSED MY FAMILY DURING THAT
TIME UNTIL WE ALL SAT DOWN TOGETHER. I CAN'T EVEN
REMEMBER WHAT WE DISCUSSED, BUT I REMEMBER
FEELING A SENSE OF COMFORT, OF SAFETY, OF PEACE
AND OF LOVE. THINKING BACK ON THAT SPECIAL TIME,
I KNOW THAT GOD WAS TRULY PRESENT AT THAT MEAL."
—Amber Dolle, wife and mother[9]

opportunity to sit around the table and share not only the food, but the activity of the day with its joys and frustrations. Meals and food can certainly function as a community builder—just leave some doughnuts near the coffee machine or company water-cooler and see how quickly people gather.

There is a local diner in New Jersey where my father goes almost every morning to eat, laugh and attempt to solve great issues of the day. The cast of characters that surround him range in age and education and they joke with each other relentlessly each morning. I've gone over there on my days off and before I hit the seat, coffee is poured, the order for the ham and cheese omelet is taken and the joking begins. This small community gathers together around the table, and there is a unity and cama-raderie that would be difficult to duplicate in any other setting.

In Jesus' day who you ate with defined you more than any-thing else, for it established and affirmed your status within the community. You knew who was a member of the in-group and who was on the outside by who was allowed around the table. This applies even more so the farther one travels outside of Jerusalem, where priestly and Levitical responsibilities were ascribed at birth. It was easy to distinguish the insiders or the religious people from the outsiders by their clothing and synagogue obligations. In the small Jewish towns that are mentioned in the New Testament, the religious made their importance and position known by inclusion and exclusion around the table. This was a fraternity that made their presence felt.

I often liken the feeling one must have experienced of being on the inside or outside to the feeling in most school cafeterias. Inclusion and acceptance by the in-group is played out daily around the lunch table. If you don't think it is a reality today, even in the church, just invite the bishop over for a meal at your next parish function and watch people scramble for the seats closest to him.

Jesus doesn't play this game. He deliberately warns his disciples against it and models the acceptable behavior in the providence of his daily life. For Jesus, the kingdom he is ushering in is a kingdom where we are all welcomed around the table. He not only welcomes sinners but *aggressively goes after them!* Jesus is not embarrassed to be seen with and eat with those considered on the margins of society. For Jesus, no one is on the margins when it comes to God's saving love. All are offered the invitation to come and eat.

Thank God Jesus welcomed sinners around the table. If not, where would you and I be? Or perhaps we think that we would be on his right hand, casting an evil eye and turning up our nose at the sinful people? I'm afraid to think where I would have been in Jesus' day. There is a sense of power, prestige and entitlement when you're part of the in-group. There's a comfort level that speaks of being part of something bigger and more important than yourself that if not held in check can be used to put others down and divide rather than unite and build others up.

While I can reflect on where I might have been back in the day, it's probably a better thing that I start reflecting on where I am today. Who do I include and exclude in the providence of my daily life? God gives me many opportunities each day to decide where I stand, or "sit" rather, on the subject. I'm sure he provides those similar opportunities for you as well.

As with most things, it starts with an attitude of the heart. We may certainly not exclude people verbally or physically, but there are ways we do that in our heart. Jesus' example of aggressively going after sinners is one that should be our model. I am a member of the Missionary Cenacle Apostolate, a lay branch of an order founded by Father Thomas Judge in the early part of the last century. Being a member of this lay organization reminds me that "every Catholic is an apostle," and every Catholic has a mission. As part of the universal mission of the church, every baptized Catholic is to go out and evangelize, to do what Jesus did. This is accomplished not only by our words, but also by with whom we eat. Sharing meals and conversation can certainly communicate God's love.

In this Scripture story we are told that the scribes of the Pharisees *saw* Jesus eating. They had no idea what was said, but the very fact that he was eating with sinners, maybe even laughing and enjoying himself, communicated something important and made the Pharisees uncomfortable. I can imagine them saying to each other, "Who is this guy letting others into our club? Doesn't he know the rules?"

In this story Levi welcomes Jesus into his house, Jesus who is the visible image of the invisible God (see Colossians 1:15). So much of biblical history takes place in the home. In the same way, so much of our history is played out in the home, around the table. So too, in the church, around the eucharistic table, saints and sinners gather to be refreshed and nourished by Word and sacrament.

Mark gives us a familial detail concerning Levi, which I often overlook. Levi is son of Alphaeus. What was in the mind of Alphaeus on the day Jesus came to dine at his son's home? We can be certain that it was an honor that the townspeople and Alphaeus never forgot, nor did the early Christian community. Was Alphaeus scorned by the Pharisees and the religious leaders like his son was? Being a sinner was not only a moral judgment on the person but rather a social characterization as well. There were some occupations, such as shepherd, that didn't allow you to fully observe the Jewish law. Being a toll collector did not necessarily mean that you were dishonest, although it may have been the case, but one had to handle coins with the image of Caesar and other graven images, which would have made you not in compliance with Jewish law.

By dining in the house of Levi, Jesus communicated to Levi's family and the community that the reign of God is at hand. God desires to have table fellowship with his people. The family of Levi could see him in a new light, a light illuminated by the presence of Jesus. I'm confident that Levi saw himself in a new light as well. Not as a sinner, scorned by God, but as a son beloved by the Father.

PRAYER

Jesus, friend of sinners and outcasts, give me the eyes of faith to see you in the poor and marginalized people I meet every day. Let me see your face in the members of my family and also in the poor. Help me to reach out to them regardless of what my friends and neighbors may say. Give me a peaceful and loving heart, especially for those who don't know you. May my actions and words never keep them away from you or give cause for scandal, but rather may they see your face in me. Forgive me for those times I looked down on others in scorn instead of reaching out to them in love. I thank you for the many meals shared around the dinner table and the eucharistic table, and let me look forward to the eternal banquet in heaven with you and all of the angels and saints. Amen.

REFLECTION QUESTIONS

1. Think about a meal that was unforgettable to you. What made it so memorable? Do you remember it because it was wonderful or maybe because it was a disaster?
2. Have you ever been looked down upon for being associated with a notorious person? What was the public perception of this person? Was there a risk you took in being associated with them?
3. How would you have felt if you were Levi that day? Imagine yourself in his shoes.
4. Have you ever been pleasantly surprised by a person of whom you may have thought very little?
5. How can you and your community reach out to those who are outcast and on the margins as Jesus did?

CHAPTER CHALLENGES

- I will spend time serving the poor in my community, but also, and maybe even more importantly, I will spend time listening to their stories.
- I will pray with my family for the conversion of those who don't know the Good News of Jesus.
- I will actively reach out and invite others who are currently outside my social group to church or a community activity.

NINE

Location, Location, Location: A Home by the Sea

(Matthew 4:12–17)

Now when Jesus heard that John had been arrested, he withdrew to Galilee. *He left Nazareth and made his home in Capernaum by the sea*, in the territory of Zebulun and Naphtali, so that what had been spoken through the prophet Isaiah might be fulfilled:

"Land of Zebulun, land of Naphtali,
   on the road by the sea, across the Jordan, Galilee of the
   Gentiles—
the people who sat in darkness
   have seen a great light,
and for those who sat in the region and shadow of death
   light has dawned."

From that time Jesus began to proclaim, "Repent, for the kingdom of heaven has come near."

WHAT ARE THE THREE MOST IMPORTANT THINGS IN REAL ESTATE? Location, location, location! It would seem that Jesus made his home in Capernaum on some prime real estate. Anyone who has ever visited Capernaum would have to agree that it is a beautiful setting. Located on the northern slope of the "harp-shaped" Sea of Galilee, west of Bethsaida and South of Chorazin, the rolling hills and cool breezes of Capernaum make it easy for one to imagine Jesus there in the same setting. It was here that Jesus made his home after leaving the friendly confines of Nazareth, separating from his mother and father, striking out on the mission for which he came and proclaiming that the kingdom of heaven has come near.

I am fascinated by the phrase, "He left Nazareth and made his home in Capernaum by the sea...." We, too, experience the same excitement and perhaps anxiety Jesus might have felt when we left home and pursued a life and career apart from the home we grew up in—anxiety and excitement side by side, looking steadfastly ahead, full of hope.

✠ ✠ ✠

"**HAVE NO FEAR OF MOVING INTO THE UNKNOWN. SIMPLY STEP OUT FEARLESSLY KNOWING THAT I AM WITH YOU, THEREFORE NO HARM CAN BEFALL YOU; ALL IS VERY, VERY WELL. DO THIS IN COMPLETE FAITH AND CONFIDENCE.**"
—Pope John Paul II[10]

What did the home of Jesus look like? What was inside? The type of building material indigenous to Galilee is a black basalt rock that can be seen today if you visit the ruins of Capernaum. Jesus, the builder, could have built his own dwelling or improved on one that he called his own or shared. Most likely it was shared with extended family and the community welcomed him as one of their own.

I'm still interested, however, in the inside. To the few people who I have shared my interest with, I get little response. "It makes little difference what it looked like," they say or shrug their shoulders, give a "who knows" look and change the topic. I can understand their lack of interest, for it doesn't change who Jesus is or his salvific work on the cross and his resurrection. But just think of all the stores that cater to home interiors and furnishing. There are thousands of them around the country that help people make the insides of their homes livable and hospitable. There are even a number of TV shows that highlight home interiors and reality shows where dramatic changes are done to the inside. Or consider all the magazines that focus on the inside of homes; again it seems as if there are a hundred of them.

So what does the house of Jesus look like? From the images Jesus used in preaching the kingdom of heaven, we can assume there was a single living space with a candle on a lamp stand that illuminated the space. There was most likely a simple basin for washing and a towel nearby. I can envision a few mats and pillows on the floor to sit on. There were places to keep the plates and cups for meals. Being a carpenter or, more accurately, a stone worker, Jesus probably took great care in making the interior a hospitable place. As mentioned previously, in first-century Middle Eastern homes the manger, or feeding trough for the animals, was located inside the home as well. The remainder I must concede is a mystery.

Jesus was most likely not concerned with the beautiful view Capernaum afforded but for the people who were there and the relationships to be made. While it's said that the three most important words in real estate are location, location, location, the three most important words for ministry to be taken from examining the life of Jesus must be relationship, relationship, relationship. Regardless of what our homes look like, the relationships we form in them must speak of a relationship with Christ. We convey the good news like Jesus did through relationships. For in building relationships we earn the right to speak from our own experience. Jesus didn't put up flyers in the synagogue or hand people a pamphlet but rather took the long view and poured his life into the twelve apostles who changed the world.

We are informed that it was after the news of the arrest of John the Baptist that Jesus made the move to Capernaum and then began his public ministry to proclaim the message, "Repent, for the kingdom of heaven has come near" (Matthew 3:2; 4:17). This move was certainly a turning point for Jesus and his mission. One chapter had ended and now another begins. Any change in our lives, be it moving, changing careers, choosing new friends or saying good-bye to old ones, can be a good thing. In fact, many people look back and point to those changes as turning points in their lives. The arrest of John precipitated the move of Jesus to withdraw to Galilee and thus set into motion his public ministry.

The homes that we make may not be noted for our sense of interior design and may never be featured in a magazine, but what do they say about us? Is the presence of Jesus felt there? Is there any evidence that Jesus has also made our home his home?

We are told, "the Son of man has nowhere to lay his head" (Matthew 8:20; Luke 9:58). Perhaps we should just be happy and thankful that we have a place to lay our heads when so many of the inhabitants of the world do not. In a spirit of thankfulness we can open up our homes and hearts to those who are homeless, be they physically without a home, or more likely, in a state of homelessness, with nowhere to call home or nowhere to fit in. May our homes and hearts be places where Christ can make his home and where all those who enter say, "God is now here!"

PRAYER

Dear Lord, you made your home near the beautiful Sea of Galilee, may you now make our hearts your home. Mold and fashion us into your image so that you may increase and we may decrease. Let us not be conformed to this world's importance on outward appearance and the material trappings of success but rather transform us inwardly so that we love people and use things instead of loving things and using people. We pray for those who are transitioning from one home to another. Wherever they call home may they know that you love them and are with them every step of the journey. We ask this through Christ our Lord. Amen.

REFLECTION QUESTIONS

1. When was the last time you experienced a major or minor change in your life? Was it a frightening experience or one you looked forward to?
2. What causes you to withdraw from your home?
3. Have you ever felt a sense of homelessness? When and why?
4. Can you think of a home where you felt the Spirit of Christ? What made you feel the presence?

CHAPTER CHALLENGES

- I will donate my time, treasure or talent to an organization that helps the less fortunate build homes for families.
- I will be active in my local community and give a voice to those who do not have adequate housing or are not provided with the basic necessities of life.
- I will help financially support a person in ministry who is reaching out to others for Christ in my community or abroad.

TEN

The Home Is Where We Share Good News

(Mark 5:8–20)

For he had said to him, "Come out of the man, you unclean spirit!" Then Jesus asked him, "What is your name?" He replied, "My name is Legion; for we are many." He begged him earnestly not to send them out of the country. Now there on the hillside a great herd of swine was feeding; and the unclean spirits begged him, "Send us into the swine; let us enter them." So he gave them permission. And the unclean spirits came out and entered the swine; and the herd, numbering about two thousand, rushed down the steep bank into the sea, and were drowned in the sea.

The swineherds ran off and told it in the city and in the country. Then people came to see what it was that had happened. They came to Jesus and saw the demoniac sitting there, clothed and in his right mind, the very man who had had the legion; and they were afraid. Those who had seen what had happened to the demoniac and to the swine reported it. Then they began to beg Jesus to leave their neighborhood. As he was getting into the boat, the man who had been possessed by demons begged him that he might be with him. *But Jesus refused, and said to him, "Go home to your friends, and tell them how much the Lord has done for you, and what mercy he has shown you."* And he went away and began to proclaim in the Decapolis how much Jesus had done for him; and everyone was amazed.

THIS STORY HAS ALL THE ELEMENTS OF A STEPHEN KING NOVEL. OF ALL THE stories in the Gospels I believe that this is one of the most frightening. After almost being drowned in a raging storm, the disciples find themselves on the "other side" of the Sea of Galilee. The other side is the scary side, the Gentile side. The first person they encounter is a possessed demoniac living among the tombs, his body bruised from harming himself with stones, and on top of all that he cries out in a loud voice day and night. He identifies himself as Legion, which signifies that he is possessed by five thousand demons. Welcome to life with Jesus.

This is a miracle story that is both frightful and sad. It's sad for the fact that when Jesus asks the man's name, he doesn't answer with his birth name given by his parents, but refers to himself by way of his condition, Legion, for there were many demons that afflicted him. This man clearly has an identity problem. Yet Jesus stands toe to toe with him and the encounter will forever change the possessed man's life. It will also change those in his town and more importantly, his family and his home.

Imagine the disciples huddled together behind Jesus ready to make a beeline for the boat! Imagine Peter gradually stepping backward, inch by inch, slowly untying the rope that anchored down the boat. I can see Peter signaling to James and John with a nod of his head, "Let's get out of here!" Life with Jesus is not always predictable but one can be sure that it is always exciting.

Jesus is not afraid to confront this man, for he too is a child of God. Confused and possessed as he is, he is not his affliction. Jesus sees beyond this man's difficulties and views him as a beloved of the Father.

How are you like this possessed man? What shackles and chains hold you down? How many people in your culture lash out against society and define themselves by their problems and afflictions? How do you identify yourself? Your true identity is not as a doctor, teacher, author, victim, patient or prisoner but rather as a child of God. By virtue of your baptism you have been set free from the chains of sin and slavery. Those other identities in which the world places so much value on may be things you *do*, but they are not ultimately who you *are*.

✛ ✛ ✛

"FAMILY IS NOT JUST ONE 'COMPARTMENT IN OUR LIFE'; THE FAMILY IS THE INTE-GRATING AND EVER PRESENT REALITY. TOUCH A PERSON AND YOU TOUCH A FAMILY."
—Reverend Harold Drexler[11]

Jesus commands the unclean spirits to enter the swine, and then they all rush down a steep bank and drown in the sea. Again, imagine those disciples looking at each other and wondering what the heck they have gotten themselves into. The swine drowned in the sea, and the man was set free. The towns-people came out to see and examine him, to see if what they had heard had really happened. If what the swine herders had reported was correct, it would make sense that they were in fear, and rightfully so.

This formerly possessed man had the desire to remain with Jesus; he pleaded with Jesus to remain with him, but Jesus, for some reason, would not permit it. The man's desire to follow Jesus *then and there* is certainly one model of discipleship, but Jesus had other plans for this man. Following Jesus demands an attentive ear and heart to listen to what Jesus wants us to do and not necessarily what we may want to do for Jesus. "Go home to your friends, and tell them how much the Lord has done for you, and what mercy he has shown you." The man did as Jesus had told him. He began to proclaim what Jesus had done for him beginning in his home.

In our desire to share the Good News of Jesus and how our lives have been set free, we may set out with good intentions while not necessarily being attentive to what the Holy Spirit may be calling us to do. It can be frustrating to have this desire that seeks to express faith but no clear path in which to do so. Saint Ignatius spoke about the discernment of spirits, in which a person listens attentively to what and where God may be calling him. There are many tools that the church offers us in discerning our path. We should not be discouraged by failures born out of our enthusiasm for God, but we should use them and the counsel of others to discern our true call. Unfortunately, without this discernment, we may be drawing more attention to ourselves and our efforts rather than to God. We may fall for the allure of success in the eyes of others rather than being faithful to what God has planned for us.

Imagine the joy and relief of the healed man's mother and father, brothers and sisters, grandparents, children, friends and neighbors! He was lost and now is found. In Jesus' eyes his value never changed regardless of his possession. He knows who he is after his encounter with Jesus, and he joyfully goes and tells the Good News to his own people in the Decapolis. We can only imagine the fruit that his witness bore in the lives of others. I would have loved to have been present when he shared his story with others.

Jesus' command to the possessed man is one that may challenge us today especially when it comes to missionary work. Evangelization, the sharing of the gospel by word and deed, begins at home. It begins by sharing the good news in a way that your community understands. If you can't share the gospel with those you know and live with, how can you expect to share it abroad? If you think that a rejection of home is the Christian way, reread this story.

Evangelization is the very reason that the church exists, to proclaim the gospel. Some may say that the word "evangelization" sounds too Protestant. If this is the case, you may have a misunderstanding about who we are called to be as Catholics. If we don't speak up, who will? Faith comes by hearing the word of God. We must speak up and proclaim the gospel beginning in our homes. If we do not begin at home guess where our children will turn? To the world, materialism, consumerism, self-indulgence or to other churches that may not be proclaiming the gospel. Evangelization is an ongoing task for all Catholics. We need to be renewed ourselves in order to go out to proclaim the Good News.

What did this man say to his family? It was pretty simple I suspect. "Here was my situation: I was afflicted, an outcast, I didn't even know who I was. Jesus came into my life and changed that. I've decided to learn more about him and follow his way of reaching out to others. It's pretty simple, really."

Do you hesitate to tell your story? Do you know that you even have one? Have you ever written it down? What are you afraid of? Like the person who sows seed in the Parable of the Sower, who sows the seeds in unexpected places, places one would expect little or no growth, we need to be attentive to the Holy Spirit to share our faith with those "unexpected" people. The results may be astonishing! Jesus was willing to live a short life, but it was a life filled with meaning and purpose. The sharing of your life story and of how God entered in is the strongest testimony we have. Don't keep it to yourself. Saint Peter reminds us to always be ready to share the Good News. Saint Francis reportedly said, "Preach the Gospel at all times. If necessary, use words." Father Thomas A. Judge reminds us to be good, do good and to be a power for good. We have some good role models to follow.

In the home, Jesus commanded the possessed man to tell his story of what God did for him. It's never too late to share that Good News with your family, in *your* home. That sharing will bear fruit in your children. In turn they will bear fruit in people and homes that you may never be aware of.

PRAYER

Jesus, companion to those who are lost and possessed, send forth your Holy Spirit to your faithful disciples. Inspire us to reach out in love to those who are far from you, especially to those people whom we might not expect to respond to you. May we communicate your message of love and freedom in ways they can identify with. Give us wisdom and fortitude to reach out and not be afraid of strange and difficult situations or people because we know that you go before us. Let us never retreat from the church's mission to bear witness to your saving love. We ask this through Christ our Lord. Amen.

REFLECTION QUESTIONS

1. Think of a situation that frightened you recently. How did you react?
2. Have you ever heard someone witness and explain what Jesus has done in her life? How did you react to her testimony?
3. How did this man's life-changing encounter with Jesus have a far-reaching impact?
4. What would you say if you were called on to let people know what God has done in your life?

CHAPTER CHALLENGES

- I will step out of my comfort zone and reach out to someone who is different from me or whom I've never talked to before.
- I will begin a daily devotional or family prayer and allow time for the family to share when its witnessed God's presence during the day.
- I will be bold in my prayer life like Jesus and pray in the power of the Holy Spirit for those who are oppressed and possessed.

ELEVEN

The Home Experiences Loss and Life
(Mark 5:35–43)

While he was still speaking, some people came from the leader's house to say, "Your daughter is dead. Why trouble the teacher any further?" But overhearing what they said, Jesus said to the leader of the synagogue, "Do not fear, only believe." He allowed no one to follow him except Peter, James, and John, the brother of James. *When they came to the house of the leader of the synagogue, he saw a commotion, people weeping and wailing loudly.* When he had entered, he said to them, "Why do you make a commotion and weep? The child is not dead but sleeping." And they laughed at him. Then he put them all outside, and took the child's father and mother and those who were with him, and went in where the child was. He took her by the hand and said to her, "Talitha cum," which means, "Little girl, get up!" And immediately the girl got up and began to walk about (she was twelve years of age). At this they were overcome with amazement. He strictly ordered them that no one should know this, and told them to give her something to eat.

THIS AND THE OTHER VERSIONS OF THIS MIRACLE STORY, RECORDED IN Matthew and Luke, all mention that people laughed at Jesus. Not in the sense that Jesus was humorous, but in the sense that he was a fool. He put them *all* outside. No messing around with Jesus in this life-and-death situation. I wonder why the crowd, in the presence of the mother and father, turned their tears and wailing so quickly to jeers and laughter. I certainly find it reasonable to question their sincerity in light of the agony the parents were going through, grieving over the loss of their only daughter. Jesus knew what to do and did it with authority; he put them outside.

Home is where suffering exists for many people. Long, winding driveways, leading up to beautifully landscaped lawns and decorative houses can easily fool outsiders from the pain, loneliness and sickness within. Less extravagant houses are also not immune from abuse, sickness and death. We may want to hide the pain from the outside world and give the impression that all is well. We may be tempted to close ourselves off from family, friends and even God. Yet, here, in this story, Jesus is not afraid to enter in and get involved.

Home is also a place where we care for those family members who are not well. Patients often feel better as long as they are home, knowing that they will be cared for. The elderly often fare much better when nursing homes accent the *home* aspect over the *nursing* aspect of the facility.

This is one such story where there is real turmoil and suffering for not only the young girl and her parents but also the extended family and the village. For when one family member suffers, we all suffer to some degree. Certainly this child's father has focused his thoughts and attention on his daughter, his wife and someone who can help. No words can describe the suffering of a parent who is in this position. The mother of the little girl in this story remains silent. What words could she have spoken to describe her pain? No words escape her lips, but we can imagine the tears that must have flowed down her cheeks and soaked the bedsheets where her daughter lay.

It is into this home that Jesus enters; a home where suffering and death is tangled up in loud wailing turmoil, commotion and unseemly laughter. Jesus put the scoffers outside. He enters the home with the family and his disciples, takes the child by the hand and says to her, "Little girl, get up!" She got up, walked and ate. A family restored by the loving touch and words of Jesus. What a difference the presence of Jesus made in that home experiencing sickness and suffering.

Unfortunately, not all of our stories end that way. Death is still an ever-present reality of our lives. It touches everyone, even those with great faith. This little girl eventually did die, as we all will. Jesus' touch points to an even greater reality, namely, by his cross and resurrection the faithful will "get up" and be born to eternal life. So what are we to make of this story in which Jesus enters a home where there is death, raises a little girl to life and restores a family to health?

The phrase that strikes me the most is: "He put them outside." Jesus miraculously heals an older woman in the midst of the commotion immediately before this healing, so we know he will do it anywhere. Yet Jesus often does his healing one on one, apart from the crowds, as in the case of the blind man whom Jesus calls aside to minister to alone. (We will see the apostles healing like Jesus healed in the Acts of the Apostles; as Jesus did, so did they do.)

What are the distractions in our lives that prevent us from experiencing the healing presence of God? What are the voices of doubt and diversion that cause us to doubt God's presence and providence in the midst of suffering and pain? Do we need to take

"I CAN THINK OF SOMETHING THAT I'LL NEVER FORGET WHEN MY GRANDFATHER PASSED. I THINK EVEN THOUGH HE WAS EIGHTY-FIVE YEARS OLD AND LIVED A FULL LIFE, THE DAY HE PASSED AWAY CHANGED ME AS A PERSON SIGNIFICANTLY. I WAS AT HOME TALKING TO MY MOM ABOUT HOW ANGRY I WAS AND HOW I PRAYED AND PRAYED TO GOD TO MAKE HIM BETTER. I ASKED HER, 'HOW COME EVERY TIME I PRAY GOD DOES THE OPPOSITE OF WHAT I ASK?' I REMEMBER SHE SAID TO ME THAT GOD DID WHAT SHE HAD PRAYED FOR, THE TIMES I WAS PRAYING FOR HIM TO GET BETTER, MY MOM WAS PRAYING FOR GOD TO TAKE HIM TO HIMSELF, BECAUSE HE WAS NO LONGER LIVING A LIFE MY GRANDFATHER WOULD WANT TO BE LIVING.

"I THINK BACK NOW AND I KNOW WAS PRAYING FOR HIM TO GET BETTER FOR MYSELF BECAUSE I COULDN'T HANDLE THE THOUGHT OF HIM LEAVING. I WAS SELFISH IN THINKING THAT HE WOULD BE ALL RIGHT LIVING HIS LIFE IN THE HOSPITAL, JUST AS LONG AS I COULD SEE HIM THINGS WOULD BE FINE. I ALSO NEEDED TO REALIZE THAT THESE DECISIONS ARE NOT UP TO ME AND THAT DEATH IS PART OF LIFE. I GOT ANGRY WITH GOD BECAUSE HE WASN'T DOING SOMETHING THAT WOULD MAKE ME HAPPY. HE DID SOMETHING TO MAKE MY GRANDFATHER HAPPY... GIVING HIM PEACE AND ETERNAL LIFE."

—Melissa Dobbin[12]

time apart from the commotion and listen to God's affirming voice and surround ourselves with the affirming voices of others? Do we, like Jesus, need to put those negative voices out of our life in order to listen to the Holy Spirit speak to us?

Personally, I know that I do better in almost everything I try when there are affirming people supporting and encouraging me.

The doubters, pessimists and cynics are often destructive to what I'm trying to accomplish or communicate. For some people the negativity can be a motivating factor, but more often than not, they need to be put outside.

Jesus not only restores the life of the little girl but also restores the family and community. This little girl will most likely go on to marry and be a mother and affect the lives of her children and many others in the community. She, who was touched by Christ, went on to touch the lives of her parents and extended family. What a joy it must have been for Jesus and the disciples to witness such a transformation in this family.

Our families need the touch of Christ in good times and in bad. As Christians we are supposed to represent Christ in the providence of our daily lives. Can we touch and heal like Jesus did in this story? Can we expel those negative voices that may mock and laugh at us for being people of faith? If we are living out our faith, we will experience those negative voices and the cynics. Will we dare to be present and face suffering when we see it? It's easy to talk about it but difficult to live it. Do you ever pray that someone would reach out to one of your family members and touch their life with a kind word, some direction or guidance? Could you be an answer to that prayer of another?

Perhaps God will work through you with miraculous power and maybe God will use you to physically heal someone. It's happened before. More likely, we will experience those little healings that happen each day with those closest to us in the home or in the home of our neighbors. Recognizing sickness, suffering and pain in others is a gift from the Spirit. God still seeks those who are open to being used to heal people and families today. Put the drama and commotion outside; bring faith on the inside.

PRAYER

God of Peace, our homes are often places where there is disorder and turmoil. We invite you into our homes to bring peace and healing. Where there is death, bring new life. Where there is weeping, bring joy. Where there is confusion, bring order. Comfort us in the knowledge that we never face our perils alone, but that you are there by our side. Guard our homes from those people who might divide us or do our family harm. Blessed Mary, Mother of God, I love you and place my needs and the needs of my family before you. Watch over us and lead us to everlasting life. Amen.

REFLECTION QUESTIONS

1. Is your house usually quiet and peaceful or full of commotion and mayhem?
2. Do you have a place that you can retreat to, to get away from the commotion and stress that life often brings? If not, do you need to create a place?
3. Who were or are some of the negative voices in your life? Have they affected you throughout your life?
4. Can you think of any positive people who have been a source of encouragement to you along your journey of faith?
5. Is there a house you can think of that needs a healing presence? What can you do to bring the healing presence of Christ to that house?

CHAPTER CHALLENGES

- I will surround myself with positive people who will support me as I live out my faith, and I will affirm someone today.
- I will be supportive with my time, treasure and talent of a hospice organization that cares for the sick and dying in their homes.

- I will quiet myself each day from the distractions and negative people who abound and make time to quietly pray to hear the positive voice of God.

TWELVE

The Home Is a Place of Teaching
(Matthew 13:1–3, 36–43)

That same day Jesus went out of the house and sat beside the sea.
Such great crowds gathered around him that he got into a boat
and sat there, while the whole crowd stood on the beach. And
he told them many things in parables, saying: "Listen! A sower
went out to sow....

Then he left the crowds and went into the house. And his disci-
ples approached him, saying, "Explain to us the parable of the weeds
of the field." He answered, "The one who sows the good seed is
the Son of Man; the field is the world, and the good seed are
the children of the kingdom; the weeds are the children of the
evil one, and the enemy who sowed them is the devil; the har-
vest is the end of the age, and the reapers are angels. Just as the
weeds are collected and burned up with fire, so will it be at the
end of the age. The Son of Man will send his angels, and they
will collect out of his kingdom all causes of sin and all evildo-
ers, and they will throw them into the furnace of fire, where
there will be weeping and gnashing of teeth. Then the righteous
will shine like the sun in the kingdom of their Father. Let anyone with ears listen!

"LISTEN!" THIS IS THE FIRST AND LAST WORD OUT OF THE MOUTH OF JESUS in this story. I never realized that about this parable until recently. And what a powerful statement Jesus makes. He commands us to listen; first he says this to the crowds outside of the house and then to the disciples inside the house. A chapter or so before this parable Jesus cries out "Let anyone with ears listen!" (Matthew 11:15). As one follows along in the Gospel of Matthew we hear similar words addressed to Peter, James and John from no less a source than God himself, when Jesus is transfigured before them. "This is my beloved Son, with whom I am well pleased; *listen* to him." (Matthew 17:5, emphasis added). The first word in the prologue of Saint Benedict's Rule for monastic life is *listen*. It is a necessity for our time with God and our time in community.

I recently gave a talk about Jesus' presence in the home for a parish retreat and afterward found myself in discussion with some of the parishioners. One father impacted me deeply as he talked so lovingly about his autistic son and daughter. Their cases were not of the most severe kind of autism but the children were autistic nonetheless and learned and responded differently from other children. What impressed me about this father was his struggle to effectively communicate to his children. I admired his honesty as he spoke of his frustration in trying to deal with them at times. He immediately made the correlation to the frustration that God must experience in trying to communicate with him. With that I could relate! Here was a man, a dad, who knew frustration and tried his best to communicate in a way his children would best respond to. He also gained insight into God's love and desire to communicate with him in a way he would best understand. His task was to listen, both to God and to his children.

Jesus uses an example of a sower sowing seeds, an example that would have been very familiar to those first-century listeners. Outside the house Jesus addresses the crowds, he "sows the seed" to the masses and exposes them to the truth of the Word of God. From the boat, as the crowd pressed in on him, Jesus speaks a parable and then the crowd disperses. The disciples approached him in the house for an explanation.

Jesus was approachable. I don't think it was a coincidence that this level of comfort took place in the intimacy of a home. A home in which Jesus was present and the disciples felt comfortable approaching him and were able to go deeper in their faith with him. There have been teachers and bosses in my life whom I felt intimidated by and I would characterize my relationship to them by the word *fear*. Upon asking a question or for something to be clarified I would be demoralized and that would be the last time I ever spoke up. I walked away from the encounter feeling deflated and discouraged. Not so with Jesus.

Imagine Jesus gathering his disciples in front of him as they sat at his feet, looking directly at him and being attentive to every word he spoke. Without a doubt they had a feeling of being special because Jesus took the time to explain the parable in detail to them. In this home even Judas was welcomed and he listened attentively to the words of Jesus.

It's amazing that one of the most important teachings of Christ, namely Jesus' teaching on his body and blood in the Eucharist, needed absolutely no clarification from the crowd or the disciples. They knew exactly what Jesus was talking about. Some left. The apostles stayed but both groups completely understood what Jesus was saying concerning the Eucharist. There was apparently no need for dialogue when Christ spoke about the

✛ ✛ ✛

"OF ALL HUMAN ACTIVITIES, MAN'S LISTENING TO GOD IS THE SUPREME ACT OF HIS REASONING AND WILL."

—Pope Paul VI[13]

necessity of eating his body and blood, a teaching one might expect needed some clarification.

The Catholic church often refers to the home as the *domestic church*, the first place where the Good News is proclaimed and taught. Are the homes we live in the domestic church in reality? Are they places where Christ is welcomed and listened to? Are we as accessible as Jesus was when questioned about faith? Do we have the answers like Jesus does as we convey the gospel to our children and family through word and deed? These are some good questions to consider, for the home should be the first place where faith is taught and where parents are the primary teachers of the faith.

My years as a teacher at a Catholic high school and a Catholic university have taught me that this is not the case with so many of our young people. As good a job as I may try to do, I can never have the impact that a parent or family member has in the home. I'd like to think that I have great influence over my students in regard to their faith life. I get along well with my students and know how to communicate the faith, but if what I say as a teacher or youth minister is not backed up in the home, my words are like the seeds that spring up and then are choked off by the weeds and cares of life.

How will you listen to Jesus and model this to your family in the home? It's never too late to start and the impact of your *listening* may have ramifications that you can't even imagine. Having a daily prayer time is an excellent way to listen to Jesus. The church's ancient practice of *lectio divina*, where you read a short passage from Scripture and meditate on it, is a powerful way to let the Word of God, rich as it is, dwell in your heart and mind. Listening to good music may be a way for people to hear the Word of God even while working on the house, doing chores or driving.

Memorizing a few key or inspirational verses from the Bible is a practice I was introduced to many years ago. I cannot begin to speak of the benefit it has had in my life. Taking a quiet walk, turning off the radio when I drive and using that as my prayer time may be the only free time I have to listen in the midst of my ever-increasingly busy life. The ways in which I can listen to God are countless. I only need to find a few techniques and practices that work best for me.

Taking time out for a retreat is vital for a healthy spiritual life. Jesus himself took time away from the crowd. Maybe you have a family and small children and think that a retreat is out of the question. I would encourage you to seek out places that have mini-retreats, days of renewal. The experience of a retreat will more than likely make you a better parent, spouse and Christian. As a person who has helped lead retreats and reflection days I, too, need time away from my hands-on ministry to recharge my batteries.

Hopefully you will find that Jesus is still accessible to you today and you will be ready to go deeper in your relationship with him. While books, education and classes in theology can deepen our knowledge of God, a seeking heart and listening ears is really the only requirement to going deeper with him. Listen!

PRAYER

Heavenly Father, you never cease listening to your children's cries for help. You who are always attentive to our yearning voices give us a listening ear. Speak to us in the silence of our hearts and give us a desire for solitude where we can listen to your call. Speak to each one of us in the way we can best understand your will and forgive us for all the times we fail to take the occasion to listen. Open our ears to our brothers and sisters around us and be attentive to their needs as well. Remind us often that the home is where meaningful teaching and Christian formation take place. We ask this through Christ our Lord, under the protection of Mary, Our Lady of Grace. Amen.

REFLECTION QUESTIONS

1. Have you ever experienced the feeling that you were not listened to? How did that make you feel?
2. What were a few of the life lessons that you were taught in the home? Do you still treasure those teachings today?
3. Who in your life really listens to you? Why are they different from others with whom you engage every day?
4. How do you listen to Jesus? Is there a time of day or practice you have that better enables you to be in a position to listen? What can you do to improve your ability to listen to Jesus?

CHAPTER CHALLENGES

- I will make an effort to listen twice as much as I speak and take special care to listen to those family members who often go unnoticed.
- I will research a few of the retreat centers in my area and sign up for a retreat that may allow me time to recollect and listen to the Holy Spirit.
- I will spend fifteen minutes each day in quiet contemplation using Scripture, music or simply quieting myself and taking in God's creation.

THIRTEEN

A Home Is Where We Can Leave the Crowd Behind

(Mark 7:17–23)

When he had left the crowd and entered the house, his disciples asked him about the parable. He said to them, "Then do you also fail to understand? Do you not see that whatever goes into a person from outside cannot defile, since it enters, not the heart but the stomach, and goes out into the sewer?" (Thus he declared all foods clean.) And he said, "It is what comes out of a person that defiles. For it is from within, from the human heart, that evil intentions come: fornication, theft, murder, adultery, avarice, wickedness, deceit, licentiousness, envy, slander, pride, folly. All these evil things come from within, and they defile a person."

CROWDS CAN BE EXHILARATING, EXCITING, ELECTRIFYING AND STRESSFUL. On occasion, they can be all these things at once. I can remember attending a number of New York Rangers' hockey games as a youngster in the late 1970s with my dad and brother. During one game a fight broke out on the ice, which is not all that uncommon.

What was unusual, however, was that as the crowd rose to their feet to witness the altercation and the roar of the crowd increased to a fever pitch, I saw a man who was in a wheelchair actually stand up to watch the two players square off to fight. It's true; I saw it with my own eyes. I'm not suggesting that the man was cured of a disease, but he was able to rise from that wheelchair for an instant. The impact of a roaring crowd can certainly have a powerful effect on us and get our adrenalin flowing as it did on that man who stood up from his wheelchair in Madison Square Garden.

I participated in World Youth Day 1993 in Denver, Colorado. One thing I'll never forget, besides camping out on a tarantula farm, was the enormous crowd that camped out overnight and endured the heat of the next day in order to listen to Pope John Paul II celebrate Mass. It was an awesome experience yet chaotic because of the large crowd, meager food, scarce bathrooms and the approximate fifteen thousand people who experienced heat exhaustion. The crowd was truly united in one spirit, one body in Christ, yet the size of the crowd brought some issues to the forefront that caused some stress.

Whether it's a sold-out sporting event or a Christmas shopping trip to the mall on "Black Friday," we are always thankful when we finally leave the crowd behind and head home. Such must have been the feeling when Jesus left the crowd and entered the house with his disciples.

The disciples had just heard Jesus speak a parable to the crowd and then asked him to explain it to them in the home. They obviously felt a level of comfort in doing this and had done it in the past. Jesus, however, gives the impression by his response that he is frustrated with them, "Then do you also fail to understand? Do you not see...?" Jesus goes on to explain the parable in greater depth. His desire to teach outweighed any frustration he may have had with the crowds or the disciples' misunderstanding.

Our homes are often the same as that house Jesus entered. We desire to get away from the crowd, to be at peace, to sit in our favorite chair and relax. Nevertheless, we are confronted by questions and misunderstandings in the home, and that can be frustrating.

Jesus answers the questions posed by his disciples and the patience Jesus shows them will be replicated by the disciples as they begin their mission after the Great Commission. Saint Peter will remind his audience to give the flock a shepherd's care. No doubt Peter remembered how Jesus dealt with him in this and other instances.

✠ ✠ ✠

"LET NOTHING TROUBLE YOU, LET NOTHING FRIGHTEN YOU. ALL THINGS ARE PASSING; GOD NEVER CHANGES. PATIENCE OBTAINS ALL THINGS. HE WHO POSSESSES GOD LACKS NOTHING. GOD ALONE SUFFICES."
—The Bookmark of Saint Teresa of Avila[14]

Jesus responds to the disciples' inquiry, "All these evil things come from within, and they defile a person." The list that is recorded has some terrible and alarming sins: fornication, theft, murder, adultery, avarice, wickedness, deceit, licentiousness, envy, slander, pride, folly. It is from within that these sins destroy a person, and it follows naturally that if the person is affected so too the family; as the family goes so goes the society. When the family is broken down on a large scale, the community experiences all of these things and can become chaotic, full of fear and distrust.

This fear and distrust can also occur in the family when there isn't the Spirit of God present. Some of the deepest hurts we can experience are not from outside the home but from within. Due to pride, folly, deceit, envy and the rest of the list, families can be destroyed from within.

When the defilement or corruption takes root in the person, the family is inevitably affected. No longer is the home and family a refuge or sanctuary but rather it becomes a place where we don't want to be. In a sense it becomes a hell, a place devoid of God. Many people have experienced that in their lives and within the home. The feelings and experience of pain flows over into their careers, relationships and all whom they touch. The bitterness and resentment can take years to recognize and to heal.

It is precisely for this reason that Jesus came: to heal our "insides" and to heal the family. Only with the love of Christ, a love that sacrifices, heals and forgives, can our families experience the joy they were meant to. Only with the love of Christ can we begin to allow ourselves to accept that forgiveness and let the healing take root and spread to others.

Jesus left the crowds that day and found that inside the house there were people he loved who did not understand his message. He patiently explained the message to the disciples, and in time they established a community of people who loved like he did and who cared like he did. By our presence and patience may people recognize these qualities in us and in our church.

PRAYER

Lord Jesus Christ, refresh me with your Holy Spirit as I enter my home after a hectic day at work or with the kids. Allow me to leave the crowds behind and be renewed at home. In the midst of the cares and concerns of the world help me to build the kingdom of God. Teach me in the providence of my daily life all that you want me to understand and know so that I may build up the body of Christ on earth. Help me to remain faithful to the service for which you call me and remind me often that it is necessary at times to leave the crowd behind. We ask this in Jesus' name. Amen.

REFLECTION QUESTIONS

1. Can you think back to a time when you wanted to leave the crowd behind? When and where was it? What made you want to get out of there?
2. Where do you go to "leave the crowd behind"? Why is this place special to you?
3. Have you ever experienced the possible frustration that Jesus may have had by having those around you not understand? How did you deal with it?
4. There is the saying, "Even doctors need doctors." In light of this fact is there a friend or a person in your life who can offer spiritual direction or counseling?

CHAPTER CHALLENGES

- I will offer to babysit for a family so the parents can experience a few hours of peace.
- I will take opportunities each week to teach a virtue to my children and put that virtue into practice myself.
- I will make time for myself to be with God each day, no regrets or guilt if other, less significant things go undone.

FOURTEEN

In the Home Faith Is Restored
(Mark 7:24-30)

From there he set out and went away to the region of Tyre. *He entered a house and did not want anyone to know he was there. Yet he could not escape notice,* but a woman whose little daughter had an unclean spirit immediately heard about him, and she came and bowed down at his feet. Now the woman was a Gentile, of Syrophoenician origin. She begged him to cast the demon out of her daughter. He said to her, "Let the children be fed first, for it is not fair to take the children's food and throw it to the dogs." But she answered him, "Sir, even the dogs under the table eat the children's crumbs." Then he said to her, "For saying that, you may go—the demon has left your daughter." So she went home, found the child lying on the bed, and the demon gone."

OF ALL THE STORIES OF HEALING IN THE GOSPELS, THIS ONE HAS ALWAYS perplexed me. It seems as if the image of Jesus I have formed in my head based on other Gospel stories comes into conflict with the image of Jesus portrayed here. In the end a women's faith was undeterred, and a little girl was healed, but the way Jesus speaks throws me for a loop.

Many theologians have mentioned that Jesus' comment, "Let the children be fed first, for it is not fair to take the children's food and throw it to the dogs," is a reference to Jesus' mission being first and foremost to the Jews. It is in line with Jesus' mission to the "lost sheep of the house of Israel," the Jewish people.

✣ ✣ ✣

"DO YOU WISH TO RISE? BEGIN BY DESCENDING. YOU PLAN A TOWER THAT WILL PIERCE THE CLOUDS? LAY FIRST THE FOUNDATION OF HUMILITY."
—Saint Augustine of Hippo[15]

While this may be true, I guess it still bothers me. Jesus seems to be holding back his healing power and compassion because this woman is a gentile, a non-Jew from Syrophoenicia. I ask myself why this makes a difference. This woman shows faith, she bows at Jesus' feet, and her request is not even for herself but for her little girl. The response Jesus gives seems to be a slap in the face to this woman who is in obvious pain.

Jesus, however, may have another reason for his reluctance. This story takes place in northwest Galilee, in the region of Tyre, a typically non-Jewish area. Jesus apparently went there to get away and did not want anyone to know he was there. In the house the woman enters making her request known to Jesus, who, fully aware of her dilemma and his mission, tells her in essence that salvation is for the Jews first and then the gentiles and the rest of the world. Jesus' imagery about the children's food being thrown to dogs is better translated as "to the puppies," a softening of the image of dogs, which was regarded as a derogatory statement since the comparison to dogs was a grave insult.

This woman is fully aware of *her mission*, to help her daughter in any way possible. She comes right back at Jesus with a clever response. She builds on his statement, not denying that salvation is from the Jews but displaying faith that Jesus' power isn't only for the Jews but for all those with faith in him, the mark of a disciple.

Jesus grants her request and assures her that the demon has left her daughter. In her home she finds her daughter lying on the bed healed, the demon gone. Imagine the joy of a mother finding her daughter healed. The persistence and wit of a gentile woman impresses the Son of God to heal her daughter "out of season" as it were.

An act of healing on Jesus' part means a family restored to health. No more anguish over the health of her daughter. No more waiting patiently over her bed hoping for a cure. Finally rest for the daughter and the family.

It can be difficult to get away for rest and relaxation, particularly today in an age of cell phones and computers and personal digital assistants. These modern technologies can be both a blessing and a curse. We are constantly being told that they will make life easier, but sometimes the opposite seems to be the reality. Instead of more time for family, friends and leisure, we end up having less. There becomes less time for sitting down to a hearty meal or curling up to read a good book because someone is always trying to contact us for something "really important." With this being more the reality of our daily lives, perhaps we can sympathize with Jesus' setting out for a distant region to get away from it all if only for a little while. And here, in the home, he is interrupted with a request for healing.

Our homes can be like the one Jesus entered in the region of Tyre. We can try our best to retreat and get away from the pressures of work and life in general, but people and problems have a way of finding us. The old saying comes to mind, "I don't have to look for trouble, trouble finds me."

The story of the Syrophoenician woman can allow us to reflect on broader social justice issues. There are many current issues today, such as war, immigration, national security and healthcare, argued over in TV news shows and radio talk shows, where we hear arguments for both sides of an issue. How does reflecting on this Gospel story help to challenge or confirm your own views and beliefs? Jesus refers to the sick child as "daughter." How do we view others? Is there an *in-group* and an *out-group*? Do we allow the newspapers and talking heads on TV or the Gospel shape and form our opinion? I'll leave the answer to you.

In the end the Syrophoenician woman went home and there was a healing, her child lying in the bed, the demon gone. What joy and relief they must have felt and what joy and relief others may feel as the result of your presence in the home knowing that they are never in the out-group.

PRAYER

Lord Jesus, you nourish us with Word and Sacrament and always include us in your every thought. Increase our faith, especially during those times when we are weak, afraid, confused and lost. When we are angry with you and mystified with your plan for our lives, let this "daughter" of the Father, this woman of faith, remind us that you do care and that God's plan for us is perfect. We pray for all parents of sick children that they may be faithful to their mission and calling as parents and that you will give them the strength they need. We ask this through Jesus Christ. Amen.

REFLECTION QUESTIONS

1. Have you ever felt the need to escape and get away for a little while? What were the circumstances that surrounded that time?

2. How does it make you feel that even Jesus needed time to be alone and unnoticed? What lesson can there be for us?

3. When have you ever felt the need to intercede on behalf of another? How did it all work out? Was the intercession through prayer or physically speaking to someone on another's account?

4. What "demons" in your life can you think of that need Jesus' attention? How can you help to remove them?

CHAPTER CHALLENGES

• I will revisit the way I handle interruptions and make an effort to see people as a gift sent by God knowing that my kindness touches the person and a family.

• I will be faithful in my intercessory prayers for others.

• I will look for opportunities to reach out to those who are different than me and allow the love of God to shine through me.

FIFTEEN

The Home Is Where Disputing Disciples Are Taught

(Mark 9:30–40)

They went on from there and passed through Galilee. He did not want anyone to know it; for he was teaching his disciples, saying to them, "The Son of Man is to be betrayed into human hands, and they will kill him, and three days after being killed, he will rise again." But they did not understand what he was saying and were afraid to ask him.

Then they came to Capernaum; and when he was in the house he asked them, "What were you arguing about on the way?" But they were silent, for on the way they had argued with one another who was the greatest. He sat down, called the twelve, and said to them, "Whoever wants to be first must be last of all and servant of all." Then he took a little child and put it among them; and taking it in his arms, he said to them, "Whoever welcomes one such child in my name welcomes me, and whoever welcomes me welcomes not me but the one who sent me."

John said to him, "Teacher, we saw someone casting out demons in your name, and we tried to stop him, because he was not following us." But Jesus said, "Do not stop him; for no one who does a deed of power in my name will be able soon afterward to speak evil of me. Whoever is not against us is for us.

IT HAS BEEN SAID THAT GOOD TEACHERS HAVE THE CORRECT ANSWERS; great teachers, however, ask the right questions. They have that ability to know what their students are thinking, subsequently, the questions they ask compel the students to think about the outcome. This ability to ask good questions allows the students to come to the discovery of truth by themselves and to examine their own lives and why they are the way they are. Jesus does this in the telling of his parables and allowing the listeners to come to the truth themselves.

In this story Jesus tells the disciples some pretty bad news. It's not the first time, nor will it be the last time, that he predicts the type of death that he will endure. Jesus knows that his disciples are confused and that they misunderstand the nature of the kingdom of God. He is aware that they were arguing amongst themselves as to who was the "greatest." One might expect Jesus to lash out at them in anger, "How long do I have to put up with you! Do you not understand what being my disciple is all about?" The disciples had by this time witnessed many miracles—a deaf man having his hearing restored, a blind man regaining his sight, Peter walking on water and even the dead being raised to life, yet these disciples act as if their ears and eyes have been shut. Peter, James and John have even witnessed Jesus' Transfiguration yet return to their old ways of thinking and living.

Jesus asks the disciples a simple question that must have pierced the disciples' hearts, for their response was silence. Jesus' creative, insightful way of dealing with division in the house can be a model for our homes today. He didn't lash out at them in public, but Jesus gathers them together in the security and safety of the home.

In the home where arguments arose, Jesus sat down, a sign of his authority, and gathers the twelve together to teach them about discipleship and service. He calls over a child and embraces him. A child is the least in a family in the sense that they are truly dependent on others for everything. They are powerless, have no rank, power or authority and cannot dispense of the family's wealth. This is discipleship, to be totally dependent on God and trust in his divine providence.

+ + +

"SEE EVERYTHING, OVERLOOK A GREAT DEAL, CORRECT A LITTLE."
—Pope John XXIII[16]

I smile at the fact that Jesus knew what they were arguing about along the way. Most parents, coaches and teachers can sense when something is not right within a family or group. Perhaps the members are just too quiet, or a look in their direction brings a downward look to their faces. I don't think Jesus necessarily used divine intuition to know that something was wrong. Jesus was close by and picked up on the fact that they were arguing. This good shepherd knows his sheep.

It is in the house that Jesus called them together to teach them in word and deed about true greatness, the giving of oneself in the service to others. The family is the great school of love through sacrifice; the greater size of the family, the greater the sacrifice, the greater the need to pull together as one for the sake of the members in the family. The family is where we learn how to love, how to respect, how to pray and how to listen to each other. When these elements are present, families flourish; when they are absent, chaos ensues.

Consider all the opportunities we have each day to serve and sacrifice for our family. If these virtues are modeled in the home, they will be lived in the community and that community will flourish. When our families suffer from the disease of selfishness and self-centeredness, our homes and communities suffer likewise.

Arguing takes place in the Christian community and all religious communities in addition to the family. Questions arise: Who is superior? Who is more morally righteous? Who has done more for the community? Look at us.... We're the only ones who are faithful, who hold more power; listen to us, or else! We have religious bullies too: those in the parish who, "hold the keys of the kingdom." It's either their way or the highway. You can hear these words echoing down through the ages and maybe in your community too. Jesus knows. He gave his life for us and set down an example for us to follow and he wants us to live it out. He wasn't kidding. That's the challenge. Not to get caught up in who runs what or who knows whom but who is the most like Jesus. Reverend Jim Chern often reminds me, "Look at the people doing the work, serving. There you find Christ."

In the house where others are present, including an impressionable child, Jesus teaches his disciples an invaluable lesson about what greatness is in God's estimation, namely, service. What lesson did the child learn that day? Children have an intrinsic desire to serve; they delight in getting things for their parents and helping in the small ways, especially when they are young. They feel important when they are included in helping Mom and Dad, Grandma and Grandpa and especially helping an older sibling. In this house Jesus calls over a young child and includes him in his teaching. What a thrill that must have been for the child. I'm certain the lesson impacted him throughout his life.

Our families need to be refreshed and renewed by people with the heart for God, a heart that gives all and serves others. Children need to see this lived out in the home; then they will be a light to their friends and the salt of their neighborhood. Until then our society will continue to be misguided like those early disciples who just didn't get it—those who thought it better to be served than to serve.

Can you recall lessons you learned in childhood from the example of others in the home? So many of the lessons we learn were taught and *caught* in the home. Nobody had to tell us specifically to do this or don't do that because it was modeled in the home, in a family.

In the end the disciples got it. They were taught by the master. These followers of Christ gave their lives in service of the Good News and changed the world. By serving others and taking the position of the least you may change your family and world.

PRAYER

Jesus our teacher, instruct us in the way of humility, the little way that Saint Thérèse lived each moment of her life. Give us the strength of your servant Pope John Paul II, who followed you in faithful service throughout his life. Raise up men and women who will serve you with the zeal of Father Thomas A. Judge, who had a heart for the Trinity and the laity and with the fortitude of Blessed Pauline Von Mallinckrodt, who called women to serve and teach the least amongst us. Ignite in us the fire of the Holy Spirit, so we may emit the light of Christ wherever we are and to whomever we meet. We ask this in Jesus' name. Amen.

REFLECTION QUESTIONS

1. Jesus creatively teaches his disciples a great lesson in this story. Who are a few of the teachers in your life that made an impact on your faith life?
2. How can arguing about "who is the greatest," the sin of pride, still divide people today? Can you think of any examples where this brings division or even death?

3. What impact do you think Jesus had on that child?

4. What is the challenge for you in this story?

CHAPTER CHALLENGES

- I will take the initiative in problem solving and making peace with those around me, especially in my family.
- I will reevaluate my definition of greatness and become more childlike in my faith and disposition to others.
- I will create an environment where I can help others discover truth in a nonthreatening way.

SIXTEEN

The Home Is Where We Grow Deeper in Faith
(Mark 10:1–12)

He left that place and went to the region of Judea and beyond the Jordan. And crowds again gathered around him; and, as was his custom, he again taught them.

Some Pharisees came, and to test him they asked, "Is it lawful for a man to divorce his wife?" He answered them, "What did Moses command you?" They said, "Moses allowed a man to write a certificate of dismissal and to divorce her." But Jesus said to them, "Because of your hardness of heart he wrote this commandment for you. But from the beginning of creation, 'God made them male and female.' 'For this reason a man shall leave his father and mother and be joined to his wife, and the two shall become one flesh.' So they are no longer two, but one flesh. Therefore what God has joined together, let no one separate."

Then in the house the disciples asked him again about this matter. He said to them, "Whoever divorces his wife and marries commits adultery against her; and if she divorces her husband and marries another, she commits adultery."

MANY OF THE TITLES GIVEN TO JESUS BY THOSE HE ENCOUNTERED IN HIS travels are recorded in the Gospels. Teacher, Lord, Master and Rabbi are but a few of the familiar ones. Rarely do we think of Jesus as a theologian but rather the supreme moral teacher. We typically consider Saint Paul as the theologian or some of the saints such as Thomas Aquinas or Augustine of Hippo, whose words about God are more scholarly and cerebral. In the post-Resurrection account of Jesus traveling the road to Emmaus, Jesus explained to those on the road the verses in Scripture that refer to Jesus beginning with Moses. This is certainly a dream for any Scripture scholar—a Bible study with Jesus! This brings our attention to the fact that Jesus was a theologian and knew how to handle theological matters.

It is in the home where Jesus shows a glimpse of his exegetical skill, his ability to draw out meaning from the Bible by explaining the Scripture to his disciples. Deuteronomy 11:19 says the following in regard to the statutes of the Lord, "Teach them to your children, talking about them when you are at home and when you are away, when you lie down and when you rise." Jesus is teaching his *children* in the home.

But back to the story above, in which Jesus discusses the problem of divorce, a problem that so often disrupts and destroys the home and family in biblical times and today. Divorce plagues many homes and unfortunately Christian homes are not immune. Infidelity, addiction, financial pressures, jealousy and lack of communication are but a few of the forces that cause conflict between a husband and wife. For some it can be an embarrassing topic to discuss as well as agonizing because of the pain and hurt experienced. We are told that the Pharisees brought up the topic in order to test Jesus and perhaps to bring some division between Jesus' teaching and the great patriarch Moses. Maybe it was their way of causing Jesus to choose between the men who could grant divorce and women who were so often the victims of divorce. Either way, Jesus doesn't shy away or back down from the question. He is not afraid to publicly state his position.

What Jesus says is very revealing. He first engages them in the dialogue by asking them a question, "What did Moses command you?" After hearing their explanation, Jesus explains to them the big picture and goes back to the beginning, before Moses, before Abraham and before the flood to the very beginning of God's intended plan.

In the garden of Eden, before sin entered the world, God made clear the intention for marriage, "Therefore a man leaves his father and his mother and clings to his wife, and they become one flesh..." (Genesis 2:24). But Adam and Eve sinned, putting their way before God's way and thus missing God's unique plan for marriage. They no longer had the Spirit of God to live out the gift God had originally planned for them, and they became a part of fallen humanity.

✠ ✠ ✠

"THE BEST GIFT I GAVE MY DAUGHTERS WAS THEIR FATHER. HE DEMONSTRATES DAILY IN HIS WORDS AND ACTIONS WHAT LOVE IS. WHAT BETTER WAY IS THERE TO GAIN SOME INSIGHT INTO GOD'S UNCONDITIONAL LOVE THAN THROUGH THIS MAN'S DEEP ABIDING LOVE FOR ME AND HIS CHILDREN! HIS FAITH IS NOT SIMPLY A SUNDAY RITUAL BUT THE CORNERSTONE OF HIS CHARACTER."
—Karen Schurtz, wife, teacher and mother to three daughters[17]

Jesus explains that because of this sinful nature of humanity Moses allows divorce, but this was not God's original intention. Without the Spirit of God it is nearly impossible to live out God's intention. Jesus, by his death and resurrection, will pay the price for original sin and thus allow us to be able to live as God intended, in relationship with him. He came that we may "live life to the fullest" (John 10:10). God the Father and God the Son give us God the Holy Spirit, which is the very love of God that enables us to live and love as God loves and to follow his plan for husband and wife. Without going into too much detail, we are to love as God loves—total, free, fruitful and faithful.

It is in the house that this lesson is taught to a group of disciples who were most likely wondering the same thing. More importantly it was modeled by Jesus' own parents and affirmed by Jesus' presence at the wedding at Cana, when he performed his first miracle. Christian marriage continues to be affirmed by couples who live out this sacrament in the power of the Holy Spirit and support of the community.

While many marriages do last for better or for worse, some do not, even when a couple makes its best effort to resolve the issues at hand. This has a devastating effect on the family as well as the community and society as a whole. It can have repercussions for the family that last generations. Nevertheless, regardless of whether a couple works things out or does not, forgiveness, reconciliation, understanding and healing can also have ramifications that will positively affect the family and community for generations to come.

Jesus certainly was a theologian! The school in which he taught was not a university in Alexandria or under the shade of the Stoas in Greece but rather in a humble, simple home where he resolved misunderstandings. May we study theology and our faith in order to grow closer to Christ and to bear fruit in the home.

PRAYER

Jesus the theologian, help us to love you with our hearts and minds. Help us to employ our intelligence and assist us in grappling with difficult teachings. Aid us in understanding to what the church teaches in a secular environment, which is often confusing. Bless those who are married. May their sacramental love of each other mirror the Holy Trinity and pour over into all of their relationships. Mary, Joseph and Jesus, pray for us. Amen.

REFLECTION QUESTIONS

1. What do you think are the ingredients that go into making a good marriage?
2. Why do you think Jesus asks the Pharisees a question instead of just telling them the answer?
3. How was conflict handled in your home growing up? What would you do the same? What would you do differently? How does one handle conflict in a healthy manner?
4. Jesus is approachable in the home and the disciples feel comfortable asking him a question in the home. What areas do you need to work on in the home so that you're more like Jesus and the disciples?

CHAPTER CHALLENGES

- I will get involved in a parish ministry that supports those contemplating marriage such as pre-Cana and share my insights and wisdom with them.
- I will not neglect the study of Scripture, and I will begin a Scripture study or join with others in breaking open God's word each week.
- I will make my marriage a priority and protect it from the forces which may harm it. If I am separated from my spouse, I will look to Jesus for peace, forgiveness and healing for all those in my family and community.

SEVENTEEN

Costly Love Poured Out in the Home

(Luke 7:36–50)

One of the Pharisees asked Jesus to eat with him, and he went into the Pharisee's house and took his place at the table. And a woman in the city, who was a sinner, having learned that he was eating in the Pharisee's house, brought an alabaster jar of ointment. She stood behind him at his feet, weeping, and began to bathe his feet with her tears and to dry them with her hair. Then she continued kissing his feet and anointing them with the ointment. Now when the Pharisee who had invited him saw it, he said to himself, "If this man were a prophet, he would have known who and what kind of woman this is who is touching him—that she is a sinner." Jesus spoke up and said to him, "Simon, I have something to say to you." "Teacher," he replied, "speak." "A certain creditor had two debtors; one owed five hundred denarii, and the other fifty. When they could not pay, he canceled the debts for both of them. Now which of them will love him more?" Simon answered, "I suppose the one for whom he canceled the greater debt." And Jesus said to him,

"You have judged rightly." Then turning toward the woman, he said to Simon, "Do you see this woman? I entered your house; you gave me no water for my feet, but she has bathed my feet with her tears and dried them with her hair. You gave me no kiss, but from the time I came in she has not stopped kissing my feet. You did not anoint my head with oil, but she has anointed my feet with ointment. Therefore, I tell you, her sins, which were many, have been forgiven; hence she has shown great love. But the one to whom little is forgiven, loves little." Then he said to her, "Your sins are forgiven." But those who were at the table with him began to say among themselves, "Who is this who even forgives sins?" And he said to the woman, "Your faith has saved you; go in peace."

SOMETIMES WHEN BEGINNING A SMALL GROUP DISCUSSION, I'LL ASK people what their most noteworthy meal was and why was it significant. I ask who was present at this meal, where it was held and what the occasion was. I'm always curious as to why they think of that particular meal out of the thousands of meals they have eaten. It's a way of breaking the ice and having people reminisce about something most of them can relate to. These meals vary from a late-night trip to the diner with friends to grandiose catered affairs at fancy banquet halls. What makes the meal significant is very rarely the food served but the people around the table. Often we don't even realize that the meal at hand may turn out to be one of the most significant meals we eat. People tend to remember the last meal they had with a loved one before he suddenly passed away, or those late-night college trips to the diner or barbeque shack with friends that would soon become a thing of the past when the demands of work and family come upon them.

This meal in the house of Simon the Pharisee will turn out to be significant for those gathered around the table. They probably didn't realize it at the time of the invitation, but there is no doubt that they would never forget this feast.

Jesus is invited into Simon's house for a meal, and he accepts and takes his place at the table. In Middle Eastern culture an invitation to the home is more than a formality, it reflects your standing in the community, and any guest would be given the best of the best that the host had to offer. But no one gives Jesus these basic cultural displays of hospitality, and it doesn't go unnoticed by the others around the table. Jesus lets it go and doesn't storm out as many others would have. Simon wants to teach Jesus a lesson about what it is to be *religious,* to be a Pharisee. Humbly, Jesus doesn't protest. The other guests were most likely thinking to themselves, *Jesus will be put in his place today. We'll let this guy know how things are done around here. Jesus goes on preaching without even asking for our approval. This itinerant preacher doesn't even protest when he is denied the basic rudiments of hospitality. Maybe he's not the big threat we thought he'd be.*

What happens next must have shaken up everyone in the room. A sinful woman enters and goes directly to Jesus' feet; her tears fall on Jesus' feet, and she pours on them the ointment from her expensive alabaster jar, drying them with her hair. These actions stopped everyone in their tracks. Heads turned in double takes, conversations ceased and eyebrows raised! Not only has a "sinful woman," most likely a prostitute, entered the house, but she let down her hair publicly, which was a scandal in that day and age. A woman's hair was normally covered and was considered to be a private part of her body, only seen by her husband after she reaches puberty. No doubt every eye in that room was fixed on the exchange between Jesus and this woman.

Simon, the Pharisee, says to himself, "If this man were a prophet, he would have known who and what kind of woman this is who is touching him—that she is a sinner." Simon defines

✛ ✛ ✛

"BEING TOGETHER AS A FAMILY, SHARING A WONDERFUL
NIGHT AND CELEBRATING MY MOM'S MILESTONE BIRTHDAY
IS WHAT STANDS OUT AND WHAT I DEARLY MISS THE
MOST. MY MOM HAS SINCE PASSED AND I WILL NEVER
HAVE THE CHANCE TO SHARE THAT SPECIAL BONDING
WITH MY MOM AND DAD EVER AGAIN...NO HUGS, NO
KISSES, NO PHONE CALLS, NO LAUGHTER,
NOTHING...ONLY MEMORIES. NO MEAL CAN REPLACE THE
LOVE, AFFECTION AND LAUGHTER THAT WE, AS A FAMILY,
SHARED THAT NIGHT. MY HEART BREAKS EVERY DAY FOR
THE LOSS OF MY PARENTS; HAVING THE HAPPY MEMORY OF
THIS LAST MEAL WILL STAY WITH ME FOREVER."

—Diane Wright, loving daughter[18]

a prophet as someone who avoids sinners, but Jesus' actions reveal that a prophet not only allows sinners to touch him but also actively engages them! Jesus is more than a prophet; he is God himself, and he permits the woman to render this lavish affection to him. She has been forgiven and pours out the tool of her trade, ointment, and her very tears at the feet of Jesus.

Jesus then does something that will make this meal unforgettable; he shames Simon in his own home in the presence of his friends. Jesus tells Simon a parable about two people who owe money and asks Simon who will be more grateful in having his debt forgiven. Simon answers correctly and then Jesus lets him have it: "Do you see this woman? I entered *your* house; *you* gave me *no water* for my feet, but she has bathed my feet with her tears and dried them with her hair. *You* gave me *no kiss*, but from the time I came in she has not stopped kissing my feet. *You did not anoint my head with oil*, but she has anointed my feet with ointment" (emphasis added). Jesus then affirms her forgiveness. The woman's *pouring out* of all she has at Jesus' feet was her response to Jesus in appreciation for forgiveness received.

What a story—an invitation, appreciation, provocation, irritation, exasperation, declaration, confrontation and finally reconciliation. All this takes place in the home around the table! No wonder this story was remembered and recalled by the early Christian community. The outrage and fury of the host, Simon, at being shamed in his own home, would no doubt lead to arrest and imprisonment of Jesus. Jesus was not afraid to stand with the poor, those who were told they were cut off from the loving presence of God. Jesus spoke the truth and let the chips fall where they may.

We don't know what happened after the meal, but I'm confident Simon was in the crowd on Passover calling for Jesus' death. But imagine if Simon had turned away from his pride and said to those gathered, "Friends, I have treated my guest, Jesus, poorly. In fact, I purposely disregarded any show of hospitality toward him. Now I'm shamed of the fact that this woman, a sinner, has shown him more hospitality and love than I. Jesus, I know now that you are a man of God, and it makes me ashamed to have ever treated you this way. Forgive me. Jesus, what is this new teaching you have about God? I'm open to listening to you." What a great ending to a story. I obviously can't change the way Simon acted in the biblical story, but I can change my attitude when I am acting like Simon and begin regarding those who are invited around the table, namely everyone, as my brothers and sisters.

What about the table where we share meals and share life? Do we make the invitation to others and show them respect and dignity regardless of their social standing? Do we use the events of the day to share the good news of reconciliation to God? Can a meal that the host thought was ruined be turned into an occasion for good?

What is God calling you to "pour out" at Jesus' feet? When we gather around the eucharistic table, we have an opportunity to offer our hearts and minds to Jesus. In the sacrament of reconciliation we can pour out our sins to him. An attentive heart and ear can hear the Holy Spirit prompting us to let go and pour out whatever may be holding us back from being more fully alive. At his feet we find mercy. *Place your heart @ the alter.*

What we model around the eucharistic table will only make sense if it's first modeled around the family table, a welcoming place where we can have fellowship with family and *pour out lavishly* to one another in love and service. What if this woman's actions were what triggered Jesus to do the same with his disciples at the Last Supper? She has undoubtedly given us an example to follow.

Some of the most significant tables in my own life were, before they were removed, the ping pong tables at the school where I teach. We had a table tennis club complete with trophies, terminology and tournaments. It was a blast playing after school and during the lunch periods, when I was able to interact with students in a way that the classroom didn't allow. Other teachers and even administrators would join in and play against the students or with them in a game of doubles. The student who was often left out in the hallway would find a place in the table tennis room where she could play and laugh and, more likely than not, get beat by me! Guess who are the former students I remain closest with? Not the straight-A students but those with whom I spent countless hours building relationships around those tables. When I spoke in class, my words were authentic because these students saw me in another light. I *poured myself out* around the tables each afternoon and lunch period. The tables you find yourself gathered around may not always be eucharistic or even for dinner but they are out there if you look.

The meal in Simon's house was one for the ages and one that the Christian community recalls throughout the world and down through the generations. Let us model Jesus and this sinful woman. Humility, teaching, healing, reconciliation and a fearless speaking of the truth in love can be a part of our homes if we so desire.

PRAYER

Heavenly Father, around the table in Simon's home you welcomed sinners and shared a meal with them. You continue to do the same today. Give us the humility of this woman to pour out our hearts before you. Never permit us to look down on others whose faults may be more public than our own. Root out of us all arrogance and pride that separates us from you and one another. Come Holy Spirit, stir into flame in our hearts a passion and desire to reach out to those who have fallen away from you and use us to welcome them back around the table. We ask this through Christ our Lord. Amen.

REFLECTION QUESTIONS

1. Can you recall a memorable meal or meeting where something totally unexpected happened or someone famous entered the room? Do you remember the details?
2. Jesus views this woman differently than the Pharisees and the others gathered around the table do. Have you ever had a change of opinion about a person? Why?
3. This woman pours out the "tools of her trade" at Jesus' feet because she will no longer need them. What may Jesus be calling you to pour out at his feet? (An attitude, past sin, old habit, anger...?)
4. Has your experience of reconciliation ever radically changed the way you behave?

CHAPTER CHALLENGES

- I will show hospitality to all who enter my home, workplace and life as if I were encountering Jesus.
- I will spend one hour in eucharistic adoration each week and pour out my heart before Jesus in the Blessed Sacrament.
- I will not be swayed by what people say or by what people think of my association with "sinners."

EIGHTEEN

Two Types of Disciples in the Home
(Luke 10:38–42)

Now as they went on their way, he entered a certain village, where a woman named Martha welcomed him into her home. She had a sister named Mary, who sat at the Lord's feet and listened to what he was saying. But Martha was distracted by her many tasks; so she came to him and asked, "Lord, do you not care that my sister has left me to do all the work by myself? Tell her then to help me." But the Lord answered her, "Martha, Martha, you are worried and distracted by many things; there is need of only one thing. Mary has chosen the better part, which will not be taken away from her."

MARTHA WAS A WOMAN OF MEANS; SHE HAD A HOME. WHEN I CONSIDER the women of antiquity, I almost always think of the term *injustice*. In many places in the world today, just being born a woman is a great disadvantage. Most of these women are predestined for poverty. I won't get into the facts and figures, but if one takes a look at developing nations, one sees that it is the women and children who suffer the most. My experience teaching at Assumption College for Sisters, which has increased my contact with numerous religious orders from around the globe, has also led me to this conclusion. To paint all women this way in Jesus' day, however, would not be accurate. We see many examples in the Gospels and in the letters of Saint Paul that depict women as strong, competent and independent, who provide for the Christian community out of their own means. Martha is one such person.

In this story we read that Martha welcomes Jesus into her home and he accepts the invitation, but what happens next is the subject of numerous books and articles. Martha is distracted with her many tasks and then reproaches Mary for seemingly doing "nothing." It would be too easy to dismiss Martha as a busybody or a woman who failed to give Jesus his due honor. After all, it is Martha who addresses Jesus as "Lord" and "Messiah" and affirms that Jesus is "the resurrection and the life" (John 11:25). What is happening in this story is what happens in every family, in every home, namely, conflict born out of a sense of injustice.

✢ ✢ ✢

"A DISCOVERY OF THE IMPORTANCE OF SILENCE IS ONE OF THE SECRETS OF PRACTICING CONTEMPLATION AND MEDITATION. ONE DRAWBACK OF A SOCIETY DOMINATED BY TECHNOLOGY AND THE MASS MEDIA IS THE FACT THAT SILENCE BECOMES INCREASINGLY DIFFICULT TO ACHIEVE. JUST AS MOMENTS OF SILENCE ARE RECOMMENDED IN THE LITURGY, SO TOO IN THE RECITATION OF THE ROSARY IT IS FITTING TO PAUSE BRIEFLY AFTER LISTENING TO THE WORD OF GOD, WHILE THE MIND FOCUSES ON THE CONTENT OF A PARTICULAR MYSTERY."

—John Paul II, *Rosarium Virginis Mariae*[19]

Martha certainly has the right to claim that she is doing all the work and Mary is just sitting there. Most of us have felt that way at some point, and it's easy for that sense of injustice to turn to anger and a lashing out. For some of us it may turn to despair. "Doesn't anyone notice all the work I'm doing?" "Does God even notice?"

What are we to learn from this story about Jesus in the house of Mary and Martha? Jesus affirms that Mary has chosen the better portion, sitting at his feet and listening to him. From Mary, whom Jesus allowed to be a student at his feet, we can learn the importance of slowing down and listening. In the preceding story Jesus tells the parable of the Good Samaritan. The emphasis is placed on the action of the Samaritan, the "doing" and "getting involved." This present story emphasizes listening to Jesus. Maybe Luke placed these stories together to show the balance of work and reflection in the life of a Christian.

That still may not satisfy the issue at hand of injustice. I wonder what other possible courses of action Martha could have taken. The way she was handling the situation did not seem to be working. How might Martha have handled the conflict differently? Can we perhaps choose an alternative solution to the conflicts we encounter even when we feel we are the victims of injustice, even when we think that God doesn't seem to notice?

Martha could have kept quiet and kept working at the task at hand. She could have shown her love for Mary by allowing her undistracted time with Jesus. It would have been a real gift to her sister. Conceivably, Martha could have gotten some "alone time" with Jesus during the clean up. Martha could have "offered up" her extra load in the kitchen as a sacrifice to God. This phrase, "offer up," may seem too outdated for some of us modern Catholics, yet there is spiritual value in silently offering our pain for others.

Martha could have stopped the kitchen work and joined Mary at Jesus' feet. The meal may have been served late, but it would not have been the end of the world. While Martha wanted to give Jesus her best by way of hospitality, maybe she missed out on Jesus giving her his best?

Instead of, "Lord, do you not care that my sister has left me to do all the work by myself? Tell her then to help me," maybe we would have read, "all the while Martha prayed for her sister that the word of Jesus would dwell in her heart and mind."

This conjecture challenges me on the way I react to unjust situations. I can't control all situations, but I can control how I respond to them. I also want to make it clear that we are called to speak out against injustice. Burying things inside usually leads to bigger problems. Silence only helps the oppressor, never the victim. We should respond to injustice in a way that is an alternative to verbal lashing out, especially when a family member is involved and it affects the home.

The opportunities for a positive, prayerful response await us each day. I know that I have been in the mode of Martha more times than I'd like to admit. Our homes, like those of the early followers of Jesus, will experience conflict. To expect our homes to experience total peace and serenity is unrealistic, even when Jesus is *at home* in our house. How we handle conflict is the challenge. Our response can be healthy or unhealthy, creative or reactionary. In the end it was Mary who chose the better portion. While dealing with conflict within our homes, pray that God gives us the wisdom to choose correctly and lovingly.

PRAYER

Loving Jesus, you took the time to speak to Mary as she listened in silence. Allow us to hear your voice as we listen both in silence and in the midst of work. Give us the wisdom to know when to speak out and to know when to offer up and unite our sorrows to you. Remind us not to let our anger lead us to sin but to seek creative solutions to our daily conflicts and misunderstanding. Martha and Mary, pray for us. Amen.

REFLECTION QUESTIONS

1. Do you feel more like a Martha or Mary in your everyday life? Does this carry over into your spirituality? How so?
2. Would you have reacted any differently than Martha did if you were in her shoes?
3. What other creative ways might have Martha responded?
4. Has conflict and the way it was handled been a concern of yours lately? How might you creatively resolve it?

CHAPTER CHALLENGES

- I will visualize myself at the feet of Jesus and offer my thoughts and prayers to him and then I will take time to listen.
- I will unclutter my life so that I am not overwhelmed with trivial matters.
- I will seek out a spiritual adviser who can guide me in the spiritual life and give me some balance and direction.

NINETEEN

At Home the Teacher Takes the Initiative

(Matthew 17:24–27)

When they reached Capernaum, the collectors of the temple tax came to Peter and said, "Does your teacher not pay the temple tax?" He said, "Yes, he does." *And when he came home, Jesus spoke of it first,* asking, "What do you think, Simon? From whom do kings of the earth take toll or tribute? From their children or from others?" When Peter said, "From others," Jesus said to him, "Then the children are free. However, so that we do not give offense to them, go to the sea and cast a hook; take the first fish that comes up; and when you open its mouth, you will find a coin; take that and give it to them for you and me."

JESUS LOVED TO ASK QUESTIONS! THE VERY FIRST WORDS OUT OF JESUS' mouth in the Gospel of John are a question: "What are you looking for?" Think about that one for a while! Before we take a look at the question Jesus poses in the home, consider some of these other questions Jesus asked:

- "Who do people say the Son of Man is?" (Matthew 16:13)
- "Where is your faith?" (Luke 8:25)
- "What do you want me to do for you?" (Matthew 20:32; Mark 10:51; Luke 18:41)
- "What does it profit them if they gain the whole world, but lose or forfeit themselves?" (Luke 9:25)
- "What were you arguing about on the way?" (Mark 9:33)
- "If you lend to those from whom you hope to receive, what credit is that to you?" (Luke 6:34)
- "Which of these...was a neighbor...?" (Luke 10:36)
- "Do you see this woman?" (Luke 7:44)
- "Why do you see the speck in your neighbor's eye, but do not notice the log in your own eye?" (Matthew 7:3; Luke 6:41)
- "Are you envious because I am generous?" (Matthew 20:15)
- "And can any of you by worrying add a single hour to your span of life?" (Matthew 6:27; Luke 12:25)
- "Is there anyone among you who, if your child asks for bread, will give a stone?" (Matthew 7:9)
- "Does he not...go in search of the one that went astray?" (Matthew 18:12)
- "Who touched me?" (Luke 8:45)
- "What is your name?" (Mark 5:9; Luke 8:30)
- "Do you now believe?" (John 16:31)
- "Are you able to drink the cup that I drink...?" (Mark 10:38)
- "...do you love me?" (John 21:15–17)

Jesus' questions call for a response. It's the way in which he taught and engaged his listeners so as to help them come to the truth. In this passage, which takes place in a home, we find Jesus alone with Peter, and class is in session.

Parents develop the gift of perceiving their children's moods, their next moves, their next questions. This "sixth sense" develops more as time goes by; and children often wonder, "How did my parents know that?" I'm not sure if this is an official "gift of the Spirit," but it certainly comes in handy from time to time.

In this story we read about the collectors of the temple tax questioning Peter as to whether or not Jesus pays the temple tax. Perhaps Jesus feels as though he is tax exempt. Every Israelite over the age of nineteen was required to pay such temple tax (see Exodus 30:13, 14; 2 Chronicles 24:6; Nehemiah 10:32; 2 Kings 12:4). Compared with today's currency, one drachma was worth about forty cents or about one day's wage for the common Israelite. There are numerous assumptions as to why the tax collectors asked Peter about Jesus' tax payment, the first being that they were try-

+ + +

"LOVE FOR THE CHILDREN IS THE BEST INSTRUCTOR IN THEIR UP-BRINGING. ONLY TO ONE WHO LOVES CHILDREN MAY THEY BE ENTRUSTED. LOVE IN THE HEART, LOVE IN THE TONE OF VOICE, LOVE IN OUR CONDUCT TOWARDS THEM—THAT ATTRACTS THEM TO US AND DRAWS DOWN GOD'S BLESSING UPON US AND THEM."
—Blessed Pauline Von Mallinckrodt, founder of the Sisters of Christian Charity[20]

ing to trap Jesus so they could accuse him of disobeying the law. Maybe a more gentle supposition was that they were simply interested in Jesus' view of the temple tax since he had other views that were out of line with how Pharisaic Judaism was practiced. Regardless of the "why" of their question, it's intriguing that it was Jesus who brought the issue up first in the home.

I like how Jesus takes the initiative. Did Jesus see the encounter between Peter and the questioners, or did the omniscient Christ just know? (The Good Shepherd knows his sheep.)

Regardless, Jesus does not let a teaching moment escape. In the home he schools Peter on an important lesson that soon, as head of the church, he will have to teach others. Jesus knew the plans he had for Peter, plans that Peter could never have imagined in his wildest dreams. The church that Jesus will give Peter the keys to will have to grapple with serious questions concerning civil authorities. Matthew, the Gospel writer, wrote to a largely Jewish community, and this story would have addressed some issues that the early Christian community had in regards to paying the tax. The temple would soon be a place that Christians were no longer welcome or allowed to worship in.

The only words Peter says are, "Yes, he does," an affirmation of Jesus paying the tax. Why then does Jesus ask him the question about from where kings take their payments when we can assume Peter had already answered correctly? Jesus may have perceived a slight dilemma in Peter by his demeanor or body language. Maybe Jesus saw the questioners giving Peter a difficult time. Jesus engages him in the story and allows Peter to discover this truth for himself in the privacy of the home.

The ending of this account is a fish story like none other. Jesus not only pays his tax with a coin Peter is to find in a fish's mouth, but he also pays for Peter's.

I like the fact that Jesus took the initiative and posed the question to Peter in the home. How can you help others discover the truth creatively, not by lectures or commands but by engaging them in dialogue? How can you help them to see the truth by getting them involved in the process? In turn, how can you be challenged by the differing viewpoints of others in how they express their relationship with God? How can you be stretched in your prayer life and views so that you may discern truth? Together, with each other's help, may we all come to a deeper knowledge and love of God.

PRAYER

Jesus, Master Teacher, you know your disciples' needs even before they speak a word of it. Take the initiative in our lives and allow us to hear your voice in the little things of life. Help us to care about the people who are in our lives and to speak to them gently and with compassion as you did with Peter. Provide for our needs, be they spiritual, emotional, psychological or material. Remind us in our journey of faith to give special attention to those in our homes that we may model your love, the love of a master teacher. We ask this is Jesus' name, through the intercession of Saint John Baptist de la Salle, patron of teachers. Amen.

REFLECTION QUESTIONS

1. Who stands out as one of the best teachers in your life? What makes him or her stand out as a teacher? *Alie — mom.*
2. Has anyone ever asked you a really thought-provoking question that you still remember to this day? How did the question stir within you and cause you to really think? *Yes Priest - Do you really care?* *I asked it now are you? care!*
3. Which question of Jesus, mentioned in this chapter or elsewhere, means the most to you and why?

CHAPTER CHALLENGES

• I will learn to ask good questions that will allow others to communicate what they are really thinking and feeling.
• I will participate in a faith-sharing group that will challenge and encourage me in my understanding of God and help me to live out my faith.
• I will take the initiative in planning activities with my family that build trust and community.

TWENTY

The Home Is Where the Celebration Begins
(Luke 15:5–6; 8–9; 28–32)

"When he has found it, he lays it on his shoulders and rejoices. And when he comes home, he calls together his friends and neighbors, saying to them, 'Rejoice with me, for I have found my sheep that was lost.'...

"Or what woman having ten silver coins, if she loses one of them, does not light a lamp, sweep the house, and search carefully until she finds it? When she has found it, she calls together her friends and neighbors, saying, 'Rejoice with me, for I have found the coin that I had lost.'...

"Then he became angry and refused to go in. His father came out and began to plead with him. But he answered his father, 'Listen! For all these years I have been working like a slave for you, and I have never disobeyed your command; yet you have never given me even a young goat so that I might celebrate with my friends. But when this son of yours came back, who has devoured your property with prostitutes, you killed the fatted calf for him!' Then the father said to him, 'Son, you are always with me, and all that is mine is yours. But we had to celebrate and rejoice, because this brother of yours was dead and has come to life; he was lost and has been found.'"

Read.

LUKE 15 IS A MASTERPIECE! WE BELIEVE THAT ALL SCRIPTURE IS INSPIRED by God, and this chapter in particular is crafted in such a way that scholars have called it the "Gospel within the Gospel." Jesus tells three parables in order to not only defend his practice of eating with sinners, but he also goes on the offensive! Jesus is actually saying, "Not only do I eat with them, but I actively seek them out! It's worse than you think!" Each of these three stories has some common elements that all come together in the last parable, the Prodigal Son, or more aptly called, "the Seeking Father." One ele- *@ Home* ment common to all is that the celebration begins at home. *seeking*

The first parable Jesus tells is popularly called the parable of the lost sheep. Jesus, however, liked to refer to it as the parable of the "seeking shepherd," for he is the hero of the parable, and the emphasis is on the seeking of the shepherd rather than on the lostness of the sheep. In this short parable, which can be read in fewer than ten seconds, Jesus begins by saying, "What man among you having one hundred sheep and losing one of them would not leave the ninety-nine in the desert and go after the lost one until he finds it?" Our familiarity with this story causes us to miss what Jesus has just done by asking, "What man among you...." He challenged the pride of the Pharisees! He does this by referring to them as shepherds! A shepherd is a wonderful image of God in the Hebrew Scriptures, but for a Pharisee to be called a shepherd would have been very insulting in Jesus' day. A shepherd was an unclean profession. It was on the list of professions a person shouldn't teach his children because if he was a shepherd he was in violation of the law. Shepherds grazed other people's sheep and the sheep would eat off land that was not their own and therefore breaking the law. You would not even know where to begin to pay reparation. This point was not lost on the listening Pharisees. Jesus further rubs it in by saying that they *lost the sheep*. To our ears that doesn't sound strange, but it was not the way Middle Eastern people spoke. One would never hear a Middle Eastern man say, "I missed the train," but rather, "The train left without me." The emphasis is not on the person, who would never take responsibility. Jesus knew what he was talking about.

In this parable there are one hundred sheep and one is missing in the wilderness. That's 1 percent, not too big a deal, right? Well, the shepherd takes care of other people's sheep, so he may be grazing your five sheep and your brother's seven sheep and your friend's four sheep and so on. If one is missing, the whole community is worried because if your sheep is missing that's 20 percent of your sheep, and that will affect your family. It affects the community as well because it will now have to sacrifice to make up for what you are lacking. The community members support and look out for each other. What affects one person affects the community.

When the shepherd finds the sheep after a costly search and news spreads that he has restored it to the flock, and to the community; everyone rejoices! There is a feast where the shepherd calls together his friends and neighbors, and this feast takes place in the home. It's important to understand who is being celebrated here. It is not the sheep! Feasters didn't place a little party hat on the lost sheep and have a party for it, but it was in honor of the shepherd who searched and carried back on his own shoulders the lost sheep. In the home the celebration began and the whole community gathered.

The next parable Jesus tells to the same Pharisees and scribes involves a coin lost in the house, not out in the wilderness. It is

+ + +

"THIS PRODIGAL SON IS MAN EVERY HUMAN BEING:
BEWITCHED BY THE TEMPTATION TO SEPARATE HIMSELF
FROM HIS FATHER IN ORDER TO LEAD HIS OWN INDEPEND-
ENT EXISTENCE; DISAPPOINTED BY THE EMPTINESS OF
THE MIRAGE WHICH HAD FASCINATED HIM; ALONE, DIS-
HONORED, EXPLOITED WHEN HE TRIES TO BUILD A WORLD
ALL FOR HIMSELF SORELY TRIED, EVEN IN THE DEPTHS OF
HIS OWN MISERY, BY THE DESIRE TO RETURN TO COM-
MUNION WITH HIS FATHER. LIKE THE FATHER IN THE
PARABLE, GOD LOOKS OUT FOR THE RETURN OF HIS
CHILD, EMBRACES HIM WHEN HE ARRIVES AND ORDERS
THE BANQUET OF THE NEW MEETING WITH WHICH THE
RECONCILIATION IS CELEBRATED.

"THE MOST STRIKING ELEMENT OF THE PARABLE IS THE
FATHER'S FESTIVE AND LOVING WELCOME OF THE RETURN-
ING SON: IT IS A SIGN OF THE MERCY OF GOD, WHO IS
ALWAYS WILLING TO FORGIVE. LET US SAY AT ONCE:
RECONCILIATION IS PRINCIPALLY A GIFT OF THE HEAV-
ENLY FATHER."

—Pope John Paul II, *Reconciliation and Penance*[21]

one of ten, 10 percent, much greater than the 1 percent in the
previous parable. What's more important than your animals?
Your money! Here Jesus quite deliberately uses the figure of a
woman for the image of God. In this instance she searches by
sweeping and by lighting a lamp. The dark, volcanic rock, called
basalt, is used in making houses in Galilee, which fits historically
and theologically in this parable. The woman must sweep in
order to hear the *jingle* of the coin and lights a lamp in order to

see it. The value of the coin doesn't change despite its "lostness." (My insight here is that the value of the person doesn't change in the sight of God regardless of how lost one might be.) When the coin is found in the home, she rejoices with her friends and neighbors *within the home*! The woman who found them is celebrated, not the coin.

The third parable escalates the cost even more. What's more important than your animals or money? Your family! In the culture of the Middle East it is your sons in particular, because they will care for you in your old age, and it is to them that your inheritance will fall. In this most popular of parables we will see two sons who are lost, both outside of the house. The younger one demands his inheritance while his father is still alive, something unheard of in that culture. In no other literature can scholars find reference to a son making this request. If the father is getting on in years and tells his sons he will divide his inheritance the sons should plead with their father saying something along the lines of, "No, no Father! Don't even suggest that you will pass on."

Not this son. What he breaks is not so much a law but a relationship with the father. Upon coming to his senses, he devises a plan to earn his way back to the father. The father runs to meet him. Here we have a father who acts like a mother. In the Middle Eastern culture and in parts of that world today men never run. It is undignified. An old adage states, "A man is known by his walk." From modern-day Turkey to deep in the heart of Africa, men of position walk with a nice, slow pace. It reveals to the community that they have their business affairs in order. This father runs because he knows that his son will be attacked by the men of the town. When hearing of the son's disrespect to the father, they understand that this disrespect also extends to the village. To ensure the honor of the town, they will make a vow to harm and even kill the son if he steps foot in the village. When the father greets him, he embraces him and kisses him over and over even before the son even says one word.

The father calls for the robe that the villagers will recognize as his, and calls for a ring, the authority of the father, and shoes for his feet, because only slaves went without shoes.

What the father does next is to kill the calf, which can feed up to seventy-five people. This is a community celebration, like the previous two parables. The whole community is involved in the singing and dancing because they are honoring the father, not the lost son. It is the father who received the son back with shalom, peace. This point is often missed today as it was missed by the older brother in the parable. In the home the celebration begins in honor of the father. It is consistent with the first two parables where the one who *seeks* is rewarded.

The story doesn't end here, however. Imagine yourself at the party, and it's really rocking. The father and son embrace as the people raise their glasses and dip their bread into the dishes filled with delicious stew and wonderful spices. The sound of drums echoes far into the night as the taste of meat invigorates your spirit. But as time goes by, you realize that someone is noticeably absent, the older brother. Word quickly spreads that he is refusing to enter the house! In the same way the father humbled himself and ran to his son, this father, in even more humiliation, rises in front of his guests who are there to honor him to go out to the elder son. The elder son sees himself not as a son but as a slave and views the party as a way of honoring the prodigal son instead of the rightful recipient, the father. The elder son incorrectly thinks that the fatted calf is slaughtered for the returning son. Not so! The honoree of this affair is the father who has received him with peace. The father makes his case, and we are left, as were the Pharisees and scribes, with a decision; namely, do we or don't we enter in the father's house?

The next scene, which is missing in the text, allows us to place ourselves in the story. A nice ending should go something like this: The elder son embraced his father and together they entered the house arm in arm where they were met by the younger son. In the presence of everyone the younger son stretched out his arms and embraced his brother and father and then the whole community rejoiced because the father received them both with peace and joy.

The home is certainly a place to celebrate the return of the lost. The home, the domestic church, was the place that the early Christian community welcomed new Christians and rejoiced with the new member of the body of Christ. The church is where we celebrate the Father. It is God the Father who loves like a mother, pouring himself out and giving his very life for his children. God is not like *a* father; but God is like *this* father in the parable.

When we celebrate the lives of saints, men and women who led heroic and sacrificial lives, we always remember that it is the love and mercy of God who acted through this person that is celebrated. As Saint Paul reminds us in Galatians 2:20: "[I]t is no longer I who live but Christ who lives in me...."

There can be a temptation to emphasize our return rather than our acceptance of being found when reading these parables. In the United States we do a wonderful job of celebrating people's accomplishments. It seems that on any given week there is an award show honoring a sports figure, actor or actress, musician, politician or television program. In the parable we should remember that it is the Seeker, God, we are honoring, not the lost.

Our worship experience should be similar. The emphasis must be on God and not ourselves. Those involved in the liturgy certainly can add to the celebration, but they must never be the focus of our worship. When the emphasis is put on the music, architecture or people serving instead of the worship of God, we overlook the reason we gather together. I thank God for those who share their talents at Mass, and their gifts add a great deal to the experience of worship.

How do we celebrate the Father's love in our homes? Like the woman seeking the lost coin, do we see the value in those who we might consider lost? Do we wait for the return of the lost or humble ourselves like the Father and demonstrate costly love to them? Others may think we're crazy in reaching out to the lost but that's OK; they thought the same about Christ.

As I write this, I'm sure there are family members or friends that come to mind who are "lost" in the sense that they are on the wrong path, maybe through their own foolishness or perhaps they may not even be aware that they are lost. Often when driving, I'm not even aware that I am lost until fifteen or twenty minutes go by and I realize I have no idea where I am. That may be analogous to others we see in the home or workplace, the people we care about who may not even realize that they are, in a sense, lost. It has been difficult for me as a teacher to let people go whom I know will face disappointment later on in life because they are so lost. I pray for them, teach the best I can and hope that God will bring them around sooner rather than later.

Maybe no laws were broken in this last parable but certainly relationships were, and they continue to wound our hearts today, just as surely as the father's heart was broken by both sons. By healing these relationships you may be healing a family. Maybe our friends who have gone astray have been away from family, friends or the church for a while. Like the good shepherd we must seek them and invite them into our homes or better yet into the Father's house. Can we assure them of our forgiveness and love even if they fail to acknowledge the harm done? It's easy to write about but difficult to live out. Just imagine the rejoicing in heaven and the celebration that awaits us all in the Father's house!

PRAYER

Seeking Father, you became one of us so that you could bring us back to yourself. The seeking shepherd, woman and father took the initiative to go after the lost. Give us a missionary heart to go after the lost and to reflect your love for them through our words and actions. Enable us to hear the voices of the lost so that we may speak a word of hope to them. Open our eyes to see the lost whether they are disguised in the clothes of a beggar or of a wealthy business executive. Thank you, Father, Son and Holy Spirit for seeking me when I was lost; continue to shepherd me as I trust in your guiding hand in my life. We ask this in the name of God the Father, who loves tenderly like a mother. Amen.

REFLECTION QUESTIONS

1. Can you think of any popular movies that portray the "lost and found" theme? Are there any similarities with these three parables?

2. Were you ever lost as a child and had to be found? Can you remember what it was like to be lost and then found?

3. Can you remember a time when you broke a relationship with a friend or vice versa? How did it make you feel then and what feelings, if any, do you still carry over from it?

4. How have you been found by God? Was there a specific time and place or has it been a process which has happened over a period of time?

5. The Catholic church is one that has a call for every baptized member to evangelize. How have or can you actively help bring others to Jesus? *How can I?*

CHAPTER CHALLENGES

- I will actively listen to the story of others and try to grasp a sense of their struggle or pain that involves any aspect of the faith, church or God without making any judgments.
- I will enthusiastically reach out to any member of my family who feels alienated or who has been away from the family.
- I will participate in my diocese's RCIA program and welcome into the church those who wish to become part of the community.

TWENTY-ONE

Lavish Love Poured Out in the Home of a Leper

(Mark 14:1–10)

It was two days before the Passover and the festival of Unleavened Bread. The chief priests and the scribes were looking for a way to arrest Jesus by stealth and kill him; for they said, "Not during the festival, or there may be a riot among the people."

While he was at Bethany in the house of Simon the leper, as he sat at the table, a woman came with an alabaster jar of very costly ointment of nard, and she broke open the jar and poured the ointment on his head. But some were there who said to one another in anger, "Why was the ointment wasted in this way? For this ointment could have been sold for more than three hundred denarii, and the money given to the poor." And they scolded her. But Jesus said, "Let her alone; why do you trouble her? She has performed a good service for me. For you always have the poor with you, and you can show kindness to them whenever you wish; but you will not always have me. She has done what she could; she has anointed my body beforehand for its burial.

Truly I tell you, wherever the good news is proclaimed in the whole world, what she has done will be told in remembrance of her." Then Judas Iscariot, who was one of the twelve, went to the chief priests in order to betray him to them. When they heard it, they were greatly pleased, and promised to give him money. So he began to look for an opportunity to betray him.

THIS REMARKABLE PASSAGE IN THE GOSPEL OF MARK TAKES PLACE IN A home of a man we know very little about. His name is Simon, and he is a leper who made his home in the town of Bethany, just a short walk from the city of Jerusalem. What would you be doing two days before the crucifixion? Jesus is dining with some outcasts: a leper and a woman who is extravagant in her lavish anointing of Jesus.

I wonder why Jesus wasn't in the house of Mary and Martha or in the home of Lazarus. They were disciples and close friends who lived in Bethany; they had been disciples of Jesus and are well-known to Christians today. Surely they would have opened their homes to Jesus. It seems obvious that Jesus had formed significant relationships with people who are not highlighted by the Gospel writers, people who for the most part are hidden from us, only making an appearance by name in a passage or two. Simon the leper is one such person.

One can reasonably assume that Simon still had leprosy, otherwise the Gospel writer would have mentioned it. Or they would have called him Simon, whom Jesus had healed, or maybe Simon, who was previously a leper. But this was not the case.

Leprosy was and is a very serious disease. The book of Leviticus has the regulations and procedure of what one was to do if afflicted with this disease. It was for the most part a death sentence for the person afflicted. The physical death would come in time but the other "death" was a death to the family and community. The diagnosed leper would be cut off from the family and worshiping community and would be put outside of the city walls or would have to remain on the outskirts of town. Many bones have been found on the treacherous Jerusalem to Jericho road in Israel, and many of those bones have been found to contain leprosy. It seems that those who were cut off from family, community and work opportunities would join with other lepers and rob people along this route.

Throughout Jesus' ministry he reaches out and heals people with leprosy. He actually touches these people who have this contagious disease. When they were healed, they were also restored to their former way of life. Yet there is no mention of healing in this story. I find that peculiar. Why wasn't he healed? Was the disease, which is translated as leprosy, one other than leprosy? Was Simon content with his condition? Did Jesus refuse to heal him for some unknown reason? I find it remarkable, nonetheless, that Jesus is at the table with a leper, known not only by his disease, but by his name, Simon.

What a sublime and powerful witness to the circle of marginalized people Jesus called his friends! Two days before the crucifixion, what would be going through your mind if you were Christ? I'm pretty sure that I would be drilling into the heads of the twelve apostles all those things that I taught them. For me, it would be like cramming for final exams, only I had to make sure that my students were prepared; after all, this is the last shot. Here, Jesus is reclined at table in the house of friends, friends who are marginalized by their disease and status in the community. Wouldn't you have loved to have been there!

What happens next will bring honor to this unnamed woman wherever the Good News is proclaimed: She broke open the alabaster jar and poured the ointment on Jesus' head. What a commotion this must have caused to the guests in the house of Simon. I can envision the costly perfume dripping down Jesus' face and beard; he closes his eyes, smiles and deeply breathes in the rich, aromatic fragrance that now fills the room. Ah, I can almost smell it!

No protest from the Son of Man but rather praise at her anointing and lavish attention. This woman recognized who Jesus really was and gave Jesus the abundant and generous anointing he deserved. The anger and misunderstanding in the home is quieted by Jesus the Christ, the anointed one.

> ✦ ✦ ✦
> "THE ONLY RETURN GOD REQUIRES OF US FOR ALL HIS FAVOURS IS A RETURN OF LOVE."
> —Venerable Catherine McAuley, founder of the Sisters of Mercy[22]

For Judas, this seems to be the last straw. In his apparent frustration and misunderstanding as to the kingdom of God that Jesus has in mind, he begins looking for an opportunity to betray him.

Jesus is welcome even in homes that we may not think are deserving of his presence. Jesus felt comfortable in the house of an outcast and was shown an extravagant display of affection and love. Even while I think he should have been spending time teaching his disciples, perhaps by his dining in the house of Simon the leper, Jesus is teaching us to place everything in the hands of God.

I recall the verse from the book of Revelation, "Listen, I am standing at the door, knocking; if you hear my voice and open the door, I will come in to you and eat with you, and you with me" (3:20). Jesus knocks on the door and seeks to dine with us today and enter into our lives and hearts. No sin we can imagine prevents him from knocking. What prevents us from opening up our doors to Christ? Have we been marginalized or considered a pariah by others and think that because we have been banished by others that we are banished from the loving presence of Jesus? Not so!

Have we opened the door of our heart and let him enter into our lives? Simon welcomed him in. No disease or dishonor by the community prevented Simon from quite literally opening his door to Jesus. In the home love and attention in the form of ointment were brought out and broken open in the presence of all to witness. Are our homes a place where Jesus is praised and shown equal attention? What will this say to those who enter our homes? Can we lavish attention on our guests regardless of their status or position? I recall the words of the first chapter of the Letter to the Hebrews that say we may have entertained angels in our midst. Christ still disguises himself in the face of a child, a migrant worker, the unemployed and others who may be poor or cut off in some way from society.

The family of Simon was honored that day as well as the family of this woman. Their story was told and is retold wherever the Gospel is proclaimed. What about your story? Without a doubt people will tell of your goodness and generosity as you welcome those into your home in the name of Jesus.

PRAYER

God our Father, seeking Shepherd, you stand and knock on the door of our hearts. Open our hearts, minds and ears to respond to your invitation. Knock so loud that we can't mistake the call. Teach me to listen to your voice and to recognize your voice in those who are separated from you, be they wealthy or poor. Holy Spirit, stir within me to make me bold, loving and wise in proclaiming the truth of your love for the entire world. Like the woman who broke open the jar of ointment and poured it all out, allow me to pour out all I have at your feet and offer my life to you. We ask this in Jesus' name and in the power of the Holy Spirit, giver of life. Amen.

REFLECTION QUESTIONS

1. If you were in Jesus' shoes, what would you have been doing immediately before the crucifixion?
2. Whom do you know who has opened their home to others? When have you ever opened your home or been the recipient of hospitality?
3. Why is there a fear in opening up our homes and lives to strangers? How can we live out the hospitality of Simon the Leper today?
4. How can you show Jesus lavish attention in your house?

CHAPTER CHALLENGES

- I will call or write a friend with whom I haven't kept in touch in order to reconnect our friendship.
- I will support with my time, treasure or talent an organization that brings healing to those with leprosy or other deadly diseases.
- I will ask God what I need to "pour out" at his feet, be it a past sin, a poor attitude or anything I may be holding back that affects my relationship with God, others and myself.

TWENTY-TWO

The Home Is a Place of Humble Service
(John 13:5)

Then he poured water into a basin and began to wash the disciples' feet and to wipe them with the towel that was tied around him.

BIBLICAL SCHOLARS DIVIDE THE GOSPEL OF JOHN INTO TWO MAIN SECTIONS. The first part, chapters 1–12, is often referred to as the Book of Signs while the second part, chapters 13–20, is called the Book of Glory. How does the book of Glory to begin? Would John tell of Jesus leading the disciples triumphantly into Jerusalem? Would he recall a miraculous healing performed by Jesus to attest to his divinity? Perhaps he would include a sermon of Jesus calling to mind his triumph over this world and eventual ascension into heaven surrounded by a myriad of angels! Jesus' way is not the world's way. For Jesus and his disciples glory isn't defined as attaining fame or credit for oneself, but rather, it is defined around a table, in a humble home, through a simple action of washing feet that won't soon be forgotten, which is where the Book of Glory begins.

Jesus' dramatic action around the table will be a model for all believers, and in time the disciples will understand, all that is, except Judas. Jesus knew that Judas was the one who would betray him, but that didn't stop Jesus from loving him along with the rest.

Jesus washed Judas' feet as well. After Jesus rose from the table, took off his outer garments and tied the towel around his waist, Jesus went to the outstretched feet of Judas, knelt down on his knees, sat back and looked lovingly at Judas. Jesus then cupped his hands and placed them in the cool water. He gently let the water pour over Judas' soiled feet. Jesus then reached for the towel and lifted Judas' feet one at a time. He supported each foot with one hand while tenderly drying them with the other. Glory redefined.

✢ ✢ ✢

"IT IS ABOVE ALL IN THE HOME THAT, EVEN BEFORE A WORD IS SPOKEN, CHILDREN SHOULD EXPERIENCE GOD'S LOVE IN THE LOVE WHICH SURROUNDS THEM. IN THE FAMILY THEY LEARN THAT GOD WANTS PEACE AND MUTUAL UNDERSTANDING AMONG ALL HUMAN BEINGS, WHO ARE CALLED TO BE ONE GREAT FAMILY."
—Pope John Paul II, Message for World Day of Peace, 1996[23]

Minutes after Jesus put his garments back on and reclined again at the table with his disciples, Judas would also share in the meal, rise and depart into the night with the feet that were just washed by the Son of Man. The prophet Isaiah wrote, "How beautiful upon the mountains / are the feet of the messenger who announces peace / who brings good news, / who announces salvation, / who says to Zion, 'Your God reigns'" (Isaiah 52:7). In contrast, how repulsive are the feet of the one who betrays the Son of God. How repulsive to people everywhere are feet that bring injustice, violence and death. We know how Judas' story ends: in shame, in isolation and finally in death.

While it was Judas who betrayed Christ at the Last Supper and handed him over to the religious leaders for trial and crucifixion, the other disciples don't come off too well either. Jesus washed the feet of Thomas who would later doubt the resurrection. Peter would deny that he even knew Jesus on three separate occasions only a few short hours after having his feet washed by him. According to Luke's account, immediately after Jesus instituted the Eucharist, these same disciples begin arguing about "who is the greatest" around the table, yet he washed their feet anyway. In the end, all those who had their feet washed by Jesus around the table abandoned him, all except the beloved disciple, John.

After the descent of the Holy Spirit, the apostles who had abandoned Christ, with those same feet, would walk the earth and change the world by spreading the Good News. The Holy Spirit would be sent to all who believe to give us the power to live and love like Jesus. We are believers today thanks in part to the apostles' witness and to their evangelistic efforts.

Of all the places Jesus could have given this example of love and service he chose to do so in a home. His words about love were backed up by his example around the table. Are our homes much different? We witness every day to what we believe by how we act, whether we seek to be served, honored and loved or we choose to serve, honor and love. Like the students and disciples of Jesus, people around us might not always get it. Our example of living like Christ and being the "foot washers" of others may be missed at first. It can be a thankless task to love like Christ by serving others. That should never stop us from serving. The question we need to ask ourselves is, "How am I like Christ?" not "What do others think of me?"

How can we begin to serve others in our homes and then bring that service to the world? When we serve a person, we serve a family. The person who receives our smile, our sacrifice or our love brings that back to a family. I'm convinced that it makes a difference.

The ways that we can live out the example of foot washing will vary from person to person and situation to situation, but any child or adult can begin today. It can start with redefining what "glory" really is in the eyes of God and in reading and meditating on this story. We are constantly bombarded with messages from the media that our beauty, minds, physical ability and power to control others are what are important, but I have found that prayers to God for opportunities to love as God loves are answered almost immediately.

The Book of Glory, in John's Gospel, begins not with a crown of gold and a storehouse of riches, but with a towel and basin. How will your book of glory begin? A good place to start is in the home.

PRAYER

My Lord, it can be so difficult to live and love as you did. There are people I meet who annoy me and others who ignore my simple acts and words of kindness. Help me not to be discouraged and to bear in mind that you never turn your back on me during those times that I am annoying and self-centered. Slow me down, Lord, slow me down. Remind me that true glory is summed up in a towel and a basin of water and not in the transitory, short- lived nonsense that popular culture tells us is glory. Lead me especially to those people who need most your touch and care, by my actions may they glimpse your presence in me. We ask this through Christ our Lord. Amen.

REFLECTION QUESTIONS

1. Can you think back to a time when someone did an extraordinary act of kindness for you? How did it make you feel?
2. Have you ever been put in a position where you felt the work was below you? How did you react? Were you angry or resentful or did you quietly do the work assigned?
3. What are a few of the ways that our culture goes against the teachings of Christ?
4. What does it mean to be a "foot washer" at home and in the marketplace?

CHAPTER CHALLENGES

- I will post a quote each week on the refrigerator or prominent place from Scripture, a saint or a famous person that speaks of service to others.
- I will place a towel and basin under the crucifix to remind me and my family what true love is.
- I will model Jesus' behavior and wash the feet of my children and spouse during Holy Week.

TWENTY-THREE

The Home Is Where We Celebrate With Christ

(Luke 22:7–23)

Then came the day of Unleavened Bread, on which the Passover lamb had to be sacrificed. So Jesus sent Peter and John, saying, "Go and prepare the Passover meal for us that we may eat it." They asked him, "Where do you want us to make preparations for it?" "Listen," he said to them, "when you have entered the city, a man carrying a jar of water will meet you; *follow him into the house he enters and say to the owner of the house,* 'The teacher asks you, "Where is the guest room, where I may eat the Passover with my disciples?"' He will show you a large room upstairs, already furnished. Make preparations for us there." So they went and found everything as he had told them; and they prepared the Passover meal.

When the hour came, he took his place at the table, and the apostles with him. He said to them, "I have eagerly desired to eat this Passover with you before I suffer; for I tell you, I will not eat it until it is fulfilled in the kingdom of God." Then he took a cup, and after giving thanks he said, "Take this and divide it among yourselves; for I tell you that from now on I will not drink of the fruit of the vine until the kingdom of God comes." Then he took a loaf of bread, and when he had given thanks, he broke it and gave it to them, saying, "This is my body, which is given for you. Do this in remembrance of me." And he did the same with the cup after supper, saying, "This cup that is poured out for you is the new covenant in my blood. But see, the one who betrays me is with me, and his hand is on the table. For the Son of Man is going as it has been determined, but woe to that one by whom he is betrayed!" Then they began to ask one another which one of them it could be who would do this.

PERHAPS THE MOST SIGNIFICANT ACTION THAT JESUS PERFORMS OUTSIDE of the crucifixion takes place in the home of an unnamed, unfamiliar person, in an upper guest room. In Luke 9:58 Jesus declares that, "Foxes have holes, and birds of the air have nests; but the Son of Man has nowhere to lay his head." It seems that the Son of Man had no home of his own to celebrate the Passover. No home of his own to transform the simple gifts of bread and wine into his precious Body and Blood. The borrowed, humble home of an unnamed friend will have to do for the Son of God.

The institution of the Eucharist is the summit of Christian worship, the way Jesus wished to be remembered and memorialized. The first Last Supper was observed and shared in a guest room and celebrated the most important of the three great historical annual festivals of the Jews. It was kept in remembrance of the Lord's passing over the houses of the Israelites (Exodus 12:13), when the firstborn of all Egyptians were destroyed. It is also called the "feast of unleavened bread" (Exodus 23:15; Mark 14:1; Acts 12:3) because during the celebration no leavened bread was to be eaten (Exodus 12:15) or even kept in the household.

✛ ✛ ✛

"THE CHURCH DRAWS HER LIFE FROM THE EUCHARIST. THIS TRUTH DOES NOT SIMPLY EXPRESS A DAILY EXPERIENCE OF FAITH, BUT RECAPITULATES THE HEART OF THE MYSTERY OF THE CHURCH. IN A VARIETY OF WAYS SHE JOYFULLY EXPERIENCES THE CONSTANT FULFILLMENT OF THE PROMISE: 'LO, I AM WITH YOU ALWAYS, TO THE CLOSE OF THE AGE' (MT 28:20), BUT IN THE HOLY EUCHARIST, THROUGH THE CHANGING OF BREAD AND WINE INTO THE BODY AND BLOOD OF THE LORD, SHE REJOICES IN THIS PRESENCE WITH UNIQUE INTENSITY. EVER SINCE PENTECOST, WHEN THE CHURCH, THE PEOPLE OF THE NEW COVENANT, BEGAN HER PILGRIM JOURNEY TOWARDS HER HEAVENLY HOMELAND, THE DIVINE SACRAMENT HAS CONTINUED TO MARK THE PASSING OF HER DAYS, FILLING THEM WITH CONFIDENT HOPE."

—Pope John Paul II, *Ecclesia de Eucharistia*[24]

The Passover celebration came afterward to denote the lamb that was slain at the feast. It was at this feast that Christians believe Jesus changed the meaning of the meal with the words, "This is my body, which is given for you. Do this in remembrance of me." Jesus gave us the greatest gift he could have given, namely himself. We have the opportunity to receive him into our lives, body, blood, soul and divinity, and in turn we can give ourselves totally to him.

Jesus gives the disciples some seemingly strange directions as to where to celebrate the Passover; directions that you or I would be perplexed at. He didn't give an address or zip code but perhaps Jesus didn't want get too specific, maybe he wanted it that way: "when you have entered the city, a man carrying a jar of water will meet you; follow him into the house...." These directions may sound odd, but remember that Jesus was a wanted man at this point. By publicly speaking the way he did, pointing out the religious leaders' hypocrisy and calling them on their indefensible treatment of the poor and marginalized, Jesus would want to keep a low profile in order to eat this meal. If everyone knew where he was celebrating the Passover, he may have been arrested before it even began.

Despite the strange directions the disciples knew where to go. They are told to go in search of, "a man carrying a jar of water." Men typically didn't carry water, which was the role of women, except in the Essene community where people went through ritual washings daily and men carried in the water.

Archaeologists have discovered what they believe to be the Essene quarter of Jerusalem; they also believe that this fringe group lived at Qumran. This is the community that left us the Dead Sea Scrolls. Their writings reveal much about their way of life and thought. The Essenes did not participate in what they believed to be the corrupted religion of the leaders of the Jewish community in Jerusalem. The Essenes were mostly celibate. The priests, or *kohanim*, adhered to purity laws far stricter than those followed by Jerusalem temple priests. The gate of the Essenes, which was cut into a preexisting city wall, gave the community access to the outside of the city and its ritual baths, or *miqva'ot*, which stood outside the city wall. Could it have been to this community that Jesus arranged a guest room? It would have provided Jesus with the easy exit out of the city he needed. He may also have had sympathizers with the Essenes, who most likely knew Jesus' disgust with many of the Pharisees and the corrupted religious practices of the day.

The disciples did as Jesus asked, finding the man, and the preparations were made. I wonder who that man was who provided the guest room. Did he realize that he welcomed the

Christ? Could he have ever imagined that his hospitality would accommodate one of the most significant events in human history? What was the reaction of his family, and how were they affected by the presence of Jesus and the disciples? In any event it was Jesus who chooses a home for his Last Supper.

Jesus had options for he would celebrate this most significant meal, but in line with Jewish custom and tradition, he celebrated it in a home, a home that welcomed him, a home not his own, a home that had been expecting him and a home of a person whose name we do not know.

I wonder how I have made others feel welcome in my home. Have I been as generous as the person who opened his heart and home to Jesus and the disciples at the first Eucharist? The challenge is certainly there for all of us to be as welcoming as that unknown person. We know that whatever we do for the least of these our brothers, we do for Christ. For some of us without a lot of extra space or for those who rent an apartment, opening up our home is a challenge.

As a Christian community how do we extend the touch and hospitality of Christ through our worship space or parish hall? Is it a place of welcome? Do those who enter our church receive a proper greeting and do we remember their names? Have we made preparations for them? All of the little details and preparations are no small matter because people will stay where they feel welcomed, and if we are to think that they will continue to worship with us, without that welcome, we do Christ an injustice.

Jesus continues to welcome disciples around the eucharistic table. It is his desire that his banquet be full. Perhaps it is in our homes that people can experience the welcome of Christ. Our hospitality to friends, neighbors and to those we may open our home to who are homeless can be a valuable way to witness to the presence of Christ. I remember vividly, as a relatively new high school teacher, the hospitality of the Wischusen family, who invited me over for dinner repeatedly. Mrs. Wischusen made it a point to serve my favorite meals when I showed up and there was always a piece of chocolate cake at the end of the meal with my name on it. As a single person, it was not only a welcome meal but a chance to interact with a family in a home, around the table and develop relationships that last to this day. I can still recall the split pea soup with ham Mrs. Wischusen made especially for me and those ham-and-cheese omelets after a round of golf with her son, Bobby. The homes we have been given are to be used for the whole body of Christ. They come to us as a gift to be shared with others. As recent natural disasters remind us, they can be taken away in an instant.

The teacher wishes to eat his supper with you and share his life with you. You don't have to follow a man carrying water to find him. Look to your home where Christ is present around the family table and then look to your local parish and join him around the eucharistic table and then become who you receive.

PRAYER

God our Teacher, Host of the great banquet, thank you for inviting us to share in the Eucharist around the table with our brothers and sisters. Open our eyes to see you fully present under the appearance of bread and wine and equally present in our neighbor. Assist us and all people in finding our way to you in expected and unexpected places and people. Draw our attention to those on the margins, those left out and those forgotten. Use our homes to welcome them, use our tables to feed them and use voices to comfort them. Remind me gently that all I have is on loan from you to be used for the good of others. Help me realize that when I reach out and touch others, I touch their families with your love as well. We ask this in the name of Jesus, our Lord and Teacher. Amen.

REFLECTION QUESTIONS

1. When have you received unexpected hospitality from another? What are the details of the story?
2. Who is someone that you can rely on for hospitality? What is it about your relationship that makes you think of this person?
3. Catholics believe in the real presence of Jesus in the Eucharist, body, blood, soul and divinity, as they say. What has been your experience with Jesus in the Eucharist? Is it a meaningful communion when you receive him at Mass?
4. How can you and your family participate in Mass so that the reception of Holy Communion is a sacred encounter?

CHAPTER CHALLENGES

- I will set aside time each week to educate myself about the Eucharist by reading or by spending time at a eucharistic adoration chapel.
- I will invite over a single friend or a coworker who often must eat alone to my home for supper.
- I will visit residents of a nursing home who often do not receive visitors.

TWENTY-FOUR

The Home Is Where We Dwell Together
(John 14:2)

In my Father's house there are many dwelling places. If it were not so, would I have told you that I go to prepare a place for you?

JESUS WAS BORN INTO A FAMILY, IN A SIMPLE HOME WHERE HE WAS SURrounded by the poor Jewish shepherds and the wealthy Gentile wise men alike. The humble beginnings of Jesus' birth would foreshadow the way he would live his life. The simplicity of his parables, the longest of which can be read in under a minute, and the humility of his speech are accessible to both scholars and children. What then, would we expect Jesus to compare heaven to? An extravagant palace or a palatial mansion? Not for Jesus. Again he surprises us with the choice of a house. This common illustration would seem consistent with who Jesus is, for the image is familial and one of simplicity.

The home was of course the central locale and focus of Jesus' ministry. So much of his teaching, healing, forgiving and eating takes place in the home that it shouldn't be all too surprising that Jesus uses it as a metaphor for heaven. Just reflect on some of the domestic references Jesus used while explaining the kingdom of God: a woman lighting a lamp to illuminate the whole room, a woman kneading dough, straining wine, sewing patches on garments, a friend visiting at midnight, a shepherd welcoming people into his house for a party at the return of the sheep that had been restored and a woman sweeping the floor seeking her lost coin and then rejoicing with friends and a party, to name a few. Jesus was more familiar with and seemingly comfortable among the people of the land, the blue collar folk, or *Am-Haretz*, as they were known, than he was with people who wore fine robes, lived in fancy palaces and ate sumptuous meals.

Jesus was all too familiar with the corruption, dishonesty and injustice that kings and kingdoms of his day were associated with. Unfortunately, injustice of this sort can be observed in every culture down through the generations. Bethlehem itself, Jesus' birthplace, was practically in the shadow of one of Herod the Great's palaces, only

✛ ✛ ✛

"WE BELIEVE THAT THE CHRISTIAN VIEW OF LIFE, INCLUDING ECONOMIC LIFE, CAN TRANSFORM THE LIVES OF INDIVIDUALS, FAMILIES, SCHOOLS, AND OUR WHOLE CULTURE. WE BELIEVE THAT WITH YOUR PRAYERS, REFLECTION, SERVICE AND ACTION, OUR ECONOMY CAN BE SHAPED SO THAT HUMAN DIGNITY PROSPERS AND THE HUMAN PERSON IS SERVED. THIS IS THE UNFINISHED WORK OF OUR NATION. THIS IS THE CHALLENGE OF OUR FAITH."
—United States Council of Catholic Bishops, *Economic Justice for All*[25]

a few miles from the manger. This palace was the third largest of Herod's palaces, which was named the Herodion, in his own honor. One can visit Bethlehem today and see in the distance the palace, which was carved out of a large mound. It stands ninety feet tall on top of a large hill and its building covered forty-five acres while the palace grounds encompassed more than two hundred acres. From the moment of his birth to the moment of his death, Jesus was surrounded by the presence of earthly kings who built monuments glorifying themselves, often by enslaving others.

Jesus spoke of his relation to God in familiar and patriarchal terms. He referred to God most frequently as Father, not "king" or "emperor." Jesus taught his followers to do likewise and spoke of himself as "Son" and to those who entrust themselves to the Father as "children of God." These children of God were to become "brothers and sisters" to each other, all familiar terms. These family relationships are the model for the Christian community, communities that view others as members of a body, members of a family. While Jesus spoke of the "kingdom of God," he wanted to make sure that his followers were not defined by the type of power and prestige exhibited by the sovereigns who control others, but rather by a humility and love which serve others.

The home is where we receive our identity, form social relations, receive nourishment and find our place in relation to others. There are, without doubt, emotional ties to the place we call home that never leave us, feelings and memories attached to times of year and friends we had. Heaven, then, should be a place we know our way around. We should feel comfortable there as we do in any place that we call home. Everyone invited will be friends, for we are all related, all sons and daughters of the Father. Imagine the nonsense and nuisances we'll do without. Imagine the reunions! Imagine the surprises of people we'll see or better yet, the surprised expressions on the faces of others who can't believe that we made it! You can almost hear the laughter already as they embrace us in disbelief.

Imagine all the people who you'll never meet on earth, greeting you and thanking you for your prayers and generosity. The time you reached out and helped another may have been the turning point in that person's life. The lives they will now touch are only because you reached out and touched him with your care and time. The money you donated to help train a teacher in a poor foreign village allowed that teacher to educate over four thousand students in her lifetime. Heaven will be full of surprises.

How will we get along with each other in heaven? Maybe it's time to reflect on how we relate to our brothers and sisters on earth. Do we forgive? Do we seek their needs before our own? Do we reach out to those in need? Do we practice the corporal and spiritual works of mercy? Do we act as ones who serve or ones who demand to be served? If we don't practice these things on earth or make an effort to do so, the place we end up may not be heaven. If we isolate ourselves from each other and ignore our brothers and sisters now, we will live in that isolation eternally. If we follow Christ according to the faith we've been given as a gift, we will truly be at home. Some of us, myself in particular, may need some more of God's grace in purgatory to prepare us and purge us from our selfishness and sin. As the sporting motto goes: You play the way you practice. Therefore, let's practice living what we're preparing for.

The relationship we have begun with Christ on earth will certainly continue in heaven. I know, of course, that we will be changed and that heaven is holy, a place where there is no stain of sin and where we cannot even begin to imagine what God has prepared for those who love him. Saint Paul mentions that we see now only dimly, as a poor reflection in a mirror. While that may be true, we can certainly reflect God's love and grace to others by our own witness.

I have heard it said that all of our good works on earth add a few more square feet to our dwelling in heaven. I'm not sure how much of that I believe. To me it just means more space I have to keep clean. Have you ever considered that the dwelling God is preparing for us may have to be shared with others? For some of us that thought may be a little frightening. We are often taught that we "possess things" and are supposed to use them for our benefit alone. After all, we earned it; we alone should use it! This is not the thought of the Middle Eastern peasants to whom Jesus was speaking. Homes are to be shared, gifts are to be brought out for the stranger and our talents are given to us for the benefit of the community.

I asked one of my African students at Assumption College for Sisters, Sister Pia Shayo, C.P.S., (a Missionary Sister of the Precious Blood) what was the biggest difference she saw between her village in Moshi, Tanzania, and the United States after her two years' experience here. Without hesitation she said, "The lack of community." She continued, "It's seems in the United States you don't know your neighbor and instead of relying on each other for your requests you pay money to strangers for your needs." That insight challenged me in my understanding of the Christian community. How attached am I to my possessions and how willing am I to share them with others or to even let others know that I am available to be of service to them?

Those who walked with Jesus opened their homes up to him. We don't know many of their names and for the people of the day it wasn't so uncommon that they would even have to mention it. As we look forward to heaven, we should also be aware that it can begin in the here and now. Our lives will witness to what we believe and after whom we model ourselves. Imagine the impact that we can have in our homes and on our family. People's lives with which we may never have direct contact may be changed forever because we welcomed their family and friends into our homes, our lives.

I hope that each day of my life is a step forward to my "fitting in" in Heaven, where Jesus assures us a dwelling place. I don't think it happens all at once, but I do believe that we can begin to make ourselves "fit in" in Heaven by loving and living like we are his children today.

PRAYER

Heavenly Father, we thank you for the gift of an eternal home, an eternal dwelling place. We keep in our prayers those who are homeless and those with homes who experience pain and suffering within them. May your loving presence be experience through symbol and action. Remind us often that the dwelling we live in and even our bodies themselves will be changed for all eternity. Help us to be generous with them both, knowing that when we open our doors and our hearts up to strangers, those in need and family members we really open them up to you. Help us to take the initiative to bring about healing in our own homes through caring and forgiveness. May those who come to our home experience your love and may our hospitality be a foreshadowing of the joy we experience in heaven. We pray this in Jesus' name. Amen.

REFLECTION QUESTIONS

1. How do you imagine heaven or your dwelling place?
2. Can you recall a peaceful dwelling or living experience that involved others? What stands out about that experience?

3. How does the idea that we will be sharing dwelling places strike you? Have you ever thought of that before?

4. What actions can you do now that may help your transition into heaven? *do unto others.*

CHAPTER CHALLENGES

⊙I will reevaluate how I view others, especially those with whom I have experienced conflict, and treat them with respect and dignity.

⊙I will plan family activities and events that solidify our identity as a family and our identity as Christians.

• I will identify people in my community who may be homeless, marginalized or maybe just alone and use my gifts, talents and home to make them feel welcome.

TWENTY-FIVE

The Home Is Where the Trinity Dwells
(John 14:23)

> Jesus answered him, "Those who love me will keep my word,
> and my Father will love them, and we will come to them and
> make our home with them."

FEW OTHER WORDS SUMMON UP THE POWERFUL EMOTIONS THAT THE word "home" does. The first thoughts that come to my mind after thoughts of my own home are scenes from the movie *The Wizard of Oz*. Most of us can picture Dorothy clicking her heels together while wearing those ruby red slippers and repeating the phrase, "There's no place like home. There's no place like home." Home is a place of joy, peace and comfort for many of us. But there is hope for people whose experience of home is unhealthy or even downright abusive. Even if our home is not perfect, it is in our hearts that the Holy Trinity wishes to take up residence and create its home.

Jesus tells us in no uncertain words that the Father and he desire to make our heart his home. He wants to dwell within us.

He wants to have that intimate union with us that we have experienced in the home in the best sense of what home is. The intimacy, if any, which we may have experienced in the home, is only a foreshadowing of the intimacy that the Holy Trinity desires to share with us. Make no mistake about it, he doesn't want to rent, he doesn't want a time-share, he wants to take up permanent residence in our heart.

When God enters into our hearts he comes as Father, Son and Holy Spirit, the Blessed Trinity. This mystery of the Trinity, which faith calls us to ascend to, is first hinted at in the book of Genesis when God refers to himself in the plural: "Let us make humankind in our image, according to our likeness" (Genesis 1:26). God refers to himself as a community of persons, a community of relationships that we are invited into. The love between the Father and Son is shared back and forth over and over, and this love is so powerful that it forms another person, the Holy Spirit, the love between the Father and Son.

The sacrament of marriage images this total self-giving love between a man and a woman that can also create new life. We image God in this selfless love. As Catholics we affirm our baptismal call to live in union with God, Father, Son and Spirit in the sacrament of confirmation. How difficult it is for one to see the Trinity moving in when there is little education or catechesis at home. Parents often relegate this responsibility of preparation to a program or retreat at church, but it is their primary responsibility to teach faith to their children. Adults who blame the church should look first to the home. There are, however, wonderful confirmation programs offered within the church. I've found that the ones that thrive have committed adults involved and a youth group for the *confirmundi* after confirmation. When there is support, prayer, the opportunity for eucharistic adoration and a youth group that engages teens relationally and spiritually, a deeper faith experience can take root.

The image that stands out to me in this verse is one taken from the book of Revelation where Jesus says, "Listen! I am standing at the door, knocking; if you hear my voice and open the door, I will come in to you and eat with you, and you with me" (Revelation 3:20). It seems clear that the desire of the Holy Trinity is to take up residence in our hearts. The invitation has been made, but it is up to us to open the door and let him in.

What that may entail is a simple "yes" spoken to God in the silence of our hearts or proclaiming that same "yes" loudly in a public demonstration of commitment to Christ. Whatever we say verbally or silently needs to be lived out in the providence of our daily lives by keeping his word. To do otherwise is not part of the package.

✦ ✦ ✦

"THE MODERN TECHNO-
LOGICAL WORLD CAN
OFFER US MANY
PLEASURES, MANY
COMFORTS OF LIFE.
IT CAN EVEN OFFER US
TEMPORARY ESCAPES
FROM LIFE. BUT WHAT
THE WORLD CAN NEVER
OFFER IS LASTING JOY
AND PEACE. THESE
ARE THE GIFTS WHICH
ONLY THE HOLY SPIRIT
CAN GIVE."
—Pope John Paul II,
Meeting with Youth, New
Orleans, 1987[26]

Jesus states that those who love him will keep his word, an external expression of reciprocated love for God. We all wish to please the one we love. It is not a burden to do so. It touches the deepest desires of our hearts. When we fail to love we don't break a set of laws or rules but rather we break a relationship. We've all experienced those hurts of being excluded and marginalized. Most likely no laws were broken but relationships were.

In order to please the one we love we need to know that person. We get to know her by spending time with her, talking and listening and being in her presence. With God it is one and the same. God comes to us as we are, whether we're broken and discouraged or hopeful and full of joy. We talk and we listen in faith, trying to grow in our relationship with him. Over time we begin to understand God's ways, God's Word and even God's silence. God is indeed the great communicator.

When a new member is added to the family, it changes the dynamic of the family and its relationships. Often it can be a cause for anxiety or joy and sometimes both at the same time. What impact should having the Trinity take up residence in our hearts have? Do we remain the same? Hopefully not! With God the Father, Son and Holy Spirit alive and active within our hearts we should love as God loves, a love that does not seek its own interest, a love that reaches out to others, a love that sacrifices for others. This type of radical love is one that is the mark of a Christian. For people will know that we are his disciples by our love for one another.

As we welcome the Trinity into our lives, we will forever be changed. Our hearts can be a welcoming place encompassing the whole world with the love of God. With God in our hearts, we can begin to love as he loves.

PRAYER

Blessed Trinity, Father, Son and Holy Spirit, come into my heart, make your home in my entire being. Fill me with the breath of life that is the love between Father and Son. Help me to know your word in order that I may keep your word. During those times when I forget your presence and darken my own life through sin, enter in even more powerfully with your light that overcomes darkness. Remind me to seek forgiveness in the sacrament of reconciliation and to make room in all aspects of my life. May your dwelling in me be a light to my family and bring peace to my home and to all who enter. Holy Trinity, stir into flame the Holy Spirit of your love to renew the face of the earth and to renew

your presence in families. We ask this through Father, Son and
Holy Spirit. Amen.

REFLECTION QUESTIONS

1. What are the first words that come to your mind when you
   hear the word "home"? *Comfort.*
2. What challenges and joys arise when a new person is added to
   a community or a new member joins the family? *Sacrifices & new giving*
3. What does it mean to keep Jesus' word? Can you describe a situation in which you kept God's word, or is there another
   meaning to this saying?
4. What images come to mind when you hear the phrase, "we will
   come and make our home in them"?
5. What responsibilities do we have in our relationship with God? *obey. "love"*
   Why does Jesus make this a requirement for loving him?

CHAPTER CHALLENGES

- I will surrender any need that I have to control people or situations and ask the Holy Spirit to lead me in all that I do.
- I will pray a Novena to the Holy Spirit nine days before
  Pentecost with my family and celebrate that feast day with family and friends.
- I will visualize the Holy Trinity entering my heart and making
  my heart its home.

TWENTY-SIX

The Home Is Where Our Blessed Mother Is Welcome
(John 19:26–27)

> When Jesus saw his mother and the disciple whom he loved standing beside her, he said to his mother, "Woman, here is your son." Then he said to the disciple, "Here is your mother." *And from that hour the disciple took her into his own home.*

MARY'S LAST WORDS OF THE GOSPEL DIRECT US TO JESUS; "DO WHATEVER he tells you." Jesus' last words direct us to Mary; "Here is your mother."

One can only imagine the view from the cross that day on Calvary. As the darkness thickened the midday sky, Christ found the strength to raise his head one last time, his vision blurred, his face and body beaten and bloodied. Though his breath became increasingly faint and his strength exhausted, Jesus addresses his mother and all the disciples from the cross. Yes, Jesus' final thoughts are of his Blessed Mother, and you. Yes, you!

Try to imagine yourself present with Jesus and his mother three years earlier during very different circumstances. Times were happier and you danced around with great exuberance and joy at a certain wedding in the small village of Cana. The new wine refreshed your parched lips and the music revitalized your spirit. The couple, whose new life together in marriage was witnessed by Jesus and Mary, now have a child of their own and the cycle of life continues for that family. Much has changed since then, however, for Jesus, his mother and the disciples.

The seemingly strange and peculiar words of Jesus, addressing his mother at the wedding in Cana as "Woman" and saying that his "hour has not yet come" (see John 2:1–11) come to mind as you gaze in bewilderment at the cross where again Jesus addresses his mother as "Woman" and there is a certain sense that this is the "hour" Jesus referred to those three short years ago.

John refers to the mother of Jesus only twice, so we can't help but make a connection between the two stories. Jesus, in his final earthly moments, did more than just provide for his mother; he provided for us. It wouldn't be too big of a stretch to say that as Jesus looked down from the cross, he saw you and me. In his desire to provide for the church, he gave us one of the greatest gifts a person could ever

✢ ✢ ✢

"BE SURE TO TURN TO THE LOVING MOTHER OF GOD. IT IS SO WONDERFUL AND SUCH A CONSOLATION THAT IN EVERY SUFFERING WE EXPERIENCE WE CAN FIND SUCH A BEAUTIFUL MOTHER IN HER. WITH HUMBLE HEART SHE STOOD UNDER THE SACRED CROSS AND REMAINED THERE SILENTLY, RECOGNIZED BY ALL AS THE MOTHER OF ONE CONDEMNED TO A PUBLIC DEATH SENTENCE. O HUMILITY— O LOVE! YOU OPEN HEAVEN!"

—Blessed Pauline Von Mallinckrodt, founder of the Sisters of Christian Charity[27]

experience, the love of a mother. What greater gift is there? Without it we are lost; with it, we have everything we need.

A mother gives life physically and spiritually. A mother's love, like all love, extends across time and space, life and death. It nurtures, touches, soothes and dwells in the heart even long after she's no longer physically present. A mother is there from the beginning. She sees, she discerns, she worries, she reflects and she gives her very life for her children. She knows sorrow and pain. Mothers always want the best for their children. So does our Mother, Mary, the Mother of all believers, who directs us to Christ.

Any brief reading of the lives of the saints past and present, including Pope John Paul II and Mother Teresa, or the martyrs and even the early church fathers reveal a real love and devotion to Mary. Consider for a brief moment all the religious orders that have a devotion to her and are named after her. Close your eyes and picture all the holy cards, paintings, stained-glass windows and statues that depict this humble Middle Eastern Jewish woman. Mary does not desire that we worship her. She directs us to her Son, the Word become flesh.

Why the devotion? What is it about Mary that draws great saints and ordinary people to her with such immense devotion? There is undoubtedly a sense of mystery about her but what is revealed through Scripture is pretty straightforward. She said "yes" to God. She gave her life completely over to the Father's will in love, total surrender. Human love attracts some, divine love attracts all. Mary was filled with this divine love. In her we find the one who gave life to Christ, the New Adam. In the same way that Jesus honored his mother and father, we walk in Jesus' steps when we honor his mother and father.

What greater presence does the church need today than the presence of Mary, our Mother? She was one like us, yet one who, in freedom, gave herself totally to the will of God. When Jesus stretched out his hands toward his disciples and said, "Here are my mother and my brothers. For whoever does the will of my Father in heaven is my brother and sister and mother" (Matthew 12:49–50). Mary was first on his list! She was the first who totally responded to grace and did the will of God in the providence of her everyday life.

Mary was present in a house with the early church in prayer (Acts 1:19), and she continues to guide disciples and the church today. Her silent witness at the cross, her being a woman of prayer as well as a woman who is lauded for her own faith can encourage us today when we face any kind of trial or tragedy.

By using the phrase "the disciple there whom he loved," the Gospel writer allows us to picture ourselves in the story for we too are beloved of the Father, sons and daughters of God. The "beloved disciple" or "the disciple Jesus loved" is used most significantly at the Last Supper, at the cross and the empty tomb. Christians today can enter into the story and be present during these events. We remember and celebrate them throughout the year and during each liturgy.

The beloved disciple brought Mary into his home. How can we bring Mary into our homes? We should probably begin with prayer, asking Jesus to reveal his mother's love for us. They say that imitation is the sincerest form of flattery, so perhaps, like Mary, we can say "yes" to God and "thy will be done" in the quiet of our hearts. We may not know for sure where that "yes" will take us or what that "yes" may mean immediately, but we can be assured that God will accomplish his will through us and that will ultimately bring us the most meaning, purpose and joy in life. God is unpredictable but never unfaithful.

While I believe that Mary's presence is realized most powerfully through our following Jesus, there are many other ways our Blessed Mother can be present in our home. Having a statue, necklace or picture of Mary can remind us of her guiding love in our lives. If you include the whole family in choosing the particular painting or image it may mean more especially to the younger members of the family. Perhaps you can place a bowl next to a small statue of Mary in your home in which family members can place the names of people and situations they are praying for or place the bowl under an icon that reveals Our Lady in relationship to Jesus. There are many wonderful prayer books and novenas, which are suitable for all ages, that direct us to Mary and help increase her loving presence.

The tradition of the church provides many formal prayers that have been prayed by Christians for centuries: The Angelus, the Regina Coeli, Hail Holy Queen and of course the Hail Mary, which come to us from Scripture, have been a source of inspiration and consolation to many. These formal prayers help us to enter into the mystery of the heart of God. My good friend, Father Dennis Berry, s.t., consistently says at the end of a blessing or prayer, "We pray for these things in the name of Jesus, under the protection of Mary, Mother of God, and Mother of the Church," which is a wonderful way to include Mary and bring her close to us as we pray.

The church gives us many days throughout the liturgical year in which to remember Mary under a number of special titles such as Our Lady of Lourdes, Our Lady of Fatima, Our Lady of Sorrows, Our Lady of Guadalupe, the feast of the Immaculate Conception and the feast of the Assumption, to name a few, in which we can honor her in a special way that will include all members of our family and can be centered around a meal.

The principal way that I have drawn close to Jesus through Mary is *praying and meditating* on the life of Jesus through the rosary. The rosary is one of the greatest gifts the church has given us. It is familiar to most everyone yet prayed by few, it would seem. While there are many books and pamphlets on the meaning of the rosary and guides to show people what to do when reciting the prayers, it is best learned by praying. For in praying the rosary we allow the joyful, sorrowful, glorious and luminous mysteries of the life of Christ to permeate our own hearts, minds and souls. It seems a bit odd at first but there is wisdom in the reciting and meditation that truly opens us up to the heart of God. There is a Dominican monastery in a neighboring town, Our Lady of the Rosary Monastery, which has the Blessed Sacrament exposed high atop a beautiful altar in a monstrance. Behind the altar one can catch an occasional glimpse of the cloistered nuns who spend their lives in prayer and in adoration. Is there a better way to honor Mary than to worship her Son?

As Christians we would do well to meditate on the cross and listen in the quiet of our hearts for the voice of God who calls to us and says, "Behold, your mother." Mary directs us to Jesus, Jesus directs us to Mary.

PRAYER

Hail Mary, full of grace, you said "yes" to God, which resulted in bringing the Word of God fully present in you. Grant us the grace to always say "yes" to God no matter the cost, no matter the sacrifice, knowing that it is God's will that brings purpose, joy and meaning in life. Give us the humble confidence that you possessed in a loving God who is unpredictable but never unfaithful. When life seems to overwhelm us, remind us of Jesus' desire to make our heart his home. Mary, mother of all disciples, pray for our families, comfort those who are ill, bring order and peace where there is strife and pray for those who have left the church; bring them back to the Eucharist, bring them back to your Son. We ask this in Jesus' name, under the protection of Mary, Mother of God, and Mother of the church. Amen.

REFLECTION QUESTIONS

1. What is your earliest childhood memory of Mary? Was there something appealing or mysterious about her? What?
2. What is your favorite depiction of Mary? Is it a painting, statue or mental image that you have formed of her?
3. Mary's last words are, "Do whatever he tells you." How can Mary assist us in listening to Jesus?
4. How can we give honor to Mary and Jesus in our homes?

CHAPTER CHALLENGES

- I will be more attentive to those who are suffering and persecuted and acknowledge them with a word of support and my very presence.
- I will honor Jesus by honoring his mother in my home. Our family will together select a Marian prayer and honor her on a special feast day around the table.
- I will make regular visits to a nursing home and perhaps adopt a patient as one of the family and let them know that they are loved and valued.

TWENTY-SEVEN

At Home Their Eyes Were Opened
(Luke 24:30–31)

> When he was at the table with them, he took bread, blessed
> and broke it, and gave it to them. Then their eyes were opened,
> and they recognized him; and he vanished from their sight.

THE GOSPEL OF LUKE BEGINS AND ENDS IN THE TEMPLE (2:27; 24:53),
but the disciples' eyes were opened in the home, around a table.
Through the breaking of the bread they recognized Jesus. I often
think I would have loved to have been there around that table
and then I realize that I can. Through the celebration of the
Eucharist we can be present with Jesus each and every time Mass
is offered. I must admit that I still need to have my eyes opened
now and again lest I lose sight of who is present in the breaking
of bread. But it is in an ordinary home that their eyes were
opened, and it's often in the home that our eyes are opened to
the presence of God.

There are a few parallels with this story that takes place at the
very end of Luke's Gospel and one of the stories that takes place

173

at the very beginning of the Bible, the fall of humanity in Genesis. In each story two people are walking with God. In the Genesis account the two people know God, eat what was forbidden and their eyes were opened. In the Emmaus story the two people didn't recognize him; they ate what was broken and given to them, and their eyes were opened. As a result Adam and Eve, focused on themselves, separated from God, could not eat as freely as before; they blamed each other and realized they were naked. In Emmaus they focused on Christ, were in communion with God, enjoyed table fellowship, formed a community and were clothed with power from on high; the Holy Spirit was given to them. The Genesis story takes place outside while the Emmaus story takes place inside.

I'm not sure if my last point is vital, for it matters little where our encounter with God takes place just as long as it does take place. We can have our eyes opened in many ways but at Emmaus it was inside of a home, at table.

Most students experience at least one or two "Aha" moments in their academic years when everything suddenly makes sense. As a teacher I hope I have been an agent of those moments when the student finally gets it. More often than not I'm afraid that I'm just one more person who is making an effort to help a person see Christ more clearly while making sure my eyes are regularly adjusted. The words of Saint Paul to the Corinthians often give me encouragement: "So neither the one who plants nor the one who waters is anything, but only God who gives the growth" (1 Corinthians 3:7). We don't have to do God's job, but God has given us a job to do.

I tell the parents of my students on back-to-school night that while I will do a good, professional job of teaching your child, what I say or do will mean very little unless it's talked about and lived out at home. The parents' involvement at home is crucial to having what I say take root or grow in their hearts. While I've witnessed God's saving power at work in the hearts of students and people with little or no faith experienced in the home, it does save most people from a great deal of heartache in the future if they have a foundation of faith.

Jesus teaches them along the way, but their eyes are opened in the home. While being the father of a newborn, I learned and experienced that a child's vision is limited at first but then begins to grow as time goes by. I've come to believe that our vision is improved over time in regard to faith; we are all in the process of having our eyes open to the reality of God. In the same way that a child connects with her mother and father, we begin to connect with God. The child recognizes the voice, aroma and touch of the parents, and she feels comfortable and secure in her parents' arms. We, too, grow in our understanding of God over time and begin to trust him more and more. There is a great freedom in that experience.

+ + +

"WHEN OUR FIRST CHILD WAS BORN, MY EYES WERE OPENED AS I WATCHED MY WIFE TAKE ON THE ROLE OF MOTHER. IT SEEMED TO COME NATURALLY TO HER AND HELPED ME TO APPRECIATE THE GIFTS GOD GIVES TO US, SOMETIMES ONLY SEEN THROUGH THE LENS OF PARENTHOOD."

—Michael St. Pierre, M.C.A., husband, father, director of campus ministry at Archbishop Curley High School, Baltimore[28]

We also need to have our eyes opened to God's presence in other places too. Do we recognize God's presence in ourselves? What do we communicate in the home when we fail to see ourselves as beloved of the Father and allow others to disrespect us and walk all over us? We are beloved in the eyes of God for who we are and not for what we may do. That experience of love transforms how we love ourselves. Do we see God's presence in our neighbor? How would others' views of themselves be changed for the good if we really viewed and treated them as created in the divine image?

My nephew, Christopher, drew me a picture when he was four years old that I still keep with me to this day. To be perfectly honest, it is not very good artistically speaking. The grass is black; I am holding something at the end of my arm because I am drawn without hands. He has no ears, nose or feet as he's standing next to me. While we are both smiling, the sun is placed about two inches from our heads and a thin blue line across the top signifies the sky. Why do I value this picture? He drew it for me after I took him miniature golfing one warm summer day and it's his remembrance of the day. You see, when you know and love the creator, you love the creation. The same is true with God. When you know and love the creator, you love the creation and can see value in it even though to others it may seem just a mess.

Our eyes need to be open to the needs of others around the world because when we know the Creator we love the creation. There are some people alive today who are in desperate need of the most basic of human necessities. The Catholic church has some of the most profound documents on social justice, but they are neglected by many people. We need to realize that our faith is not just us and Jesus, but it includes our relationship to all people everywhere, especially to those in need. We can't be all things to all people but we do have a responsibility to reach out and allow our eyes to be opened to the needs of others. One such couple who are warriors for justice are my friend David O'Brien and his wife Retzel, who, instead of accepting wedding presents for themselves at their wedding, provided a list of items and things to do that would serve the poor because they themselves are so blessed. Dave reminds me to even keep watch over where I invest my money lest I support an institution that does harm to the human person. This is just a small example of how our eyes can be opened. This type of witness begins in the home. I once overheard a parent say, "I don't mind if my child doesn't hear what I say, but he better hear what I do." I know what she means. Our actions do speak louder than words.

What we demonstrate around the dinner table can be just as important as what we do around the eucharistic table, especially for children. For around the dinner table with my family, the father sits at the head of the table with the family gathered around; we pray, eat, laugh, listen and learn. It's an easy transition to gather around the eucharistic table after gathering around the family table. We learn who we are in relationship to God and to one another, we learn our family story and we add to the conversation around the table.

PRAYER

Heavenly Father, you walked in the garden of Eden with Adam and Eve and you walked alongside those disciples on the road to Emmaus. Open our eyes so that we may recognize you in the bread and wine of the Eucharist as we walk with you on our journey of faith. Illuminate our hearts and minds to understand the words of Scripture. Thaw our hardened hearts from callousness and insensitivity; give us your heart for the poor, imprisoned and blind. Lord, remind me gently before I criticize others to remove the log from my own eye so that I may give witness to what I believe through my thoughts, actions and words. Saint Lucy, Saint Damian and Saint Raphael the Archangel, patron saints of the blind, pray for us that our eyes may be opened. We ask this through Christ our Lord. Amen.

REFLECTION QUESTIONS

1. Who has journeyed with you through life so far? Can you think of any friends who have stood by your side through the years?
2. Where are some of the places you recognize God's presence?
3. Have you ever had an "Aha" moment with God, perhaps on a retreat or while reading Scripture?
4. How can you more fully participate in the Mass?

CHAPTER CHALLENGES

• I will take fifteen minutes each day to study Scripture, perhaps read a Psalm and a portion of the Gospels each morning.
• I will participate in a Scripture study in order to break open the Word of God and allow God to speak to me through the Bible.
• I will quiet myself before Mass and ask God that my eyes and ears be open to his presence in the Word and Sacrament.

TWENTY-EIGHT

Come, Holy Spirit, in the Home
(John 20:19–23)

When it was evening on that day, the first day of the week, and the doors of the house where the disciples had met were locked for fear of the Jews, Jesus came and stood among them and said, "Peace be with you." After he said this, he showed them his hands and his side. Then the disciples rejoiced when they saw the Lord. Jesus said to them again, "Peace be with you. As the Father has sent me, so I send you." When he had said this, he breathed on them and said to them, "Receive the Holy Spirit. If you forgive the sins of any, they are forgiven them; if you retain the sins of any, they are retained."

IT'S LATE. IT'S DARK OUTSIDE. THE DISCIPLES ARE HUDDLED TOGETHER out of fear. It matters little if the fear is real or imagined. The doors are locked where they stay. This is not a common image of the post-Resurrection Christian community. This is, however, where we find the closest companions of Jesus after the Crucifixion. It's not a pretty picture to say the least, and it's one that will change dramatically in a few moments.

The disciples have experienced many highs and lows. It seems that hope is all but extinguished in the despair and fear they experience. We are informed that before this encounter with the risen Jesus, Mary of Magdala went to the tomb and saw for herself that the tomb was empty. She ran to Simon Peter and to the other disciples to announce that Jesus was not there. Peter and John went to the tomb, looked in and saw for themselves that the body was gone. Only the burial clothes remained. They returned home. Mary then has an encounter with the risen Lord and is the first to bring the good news to the disciples. Blessed are the feet of the one who brings good news.

In this dark, locked and fear-filled home Jesus enters. Jesus, the light of the world, shines in the darkness, and the darkness did not overcome it. The resurrected Lord calls the disciples his "brothers" for the first time. This is a new title for them that signifies a new relationship as they are about to be reborn with the Spirit of God. We, too, enter into this new relationship with Jesus and can rightly be called his brothers and sisters.

There are a few points worth considering surrounding this post-Resurrection appearance of Jesus. First of all, it wasn't in the temple or synagogue that Jesus appeared after the resurrection; the disciples first experience the risen Lord in, you guessed it, the home. One might even consider who Jesus would want to show himself to first. Perhaps Pilate, who condemned him to death, or the soldiers, who nailed him to the cross, might have been first on my list if I were Jesus, but no. God's ways are certainly not mine. Jesus appears to his friends in an environment where he has met them before, the confines of a home.

Secondly, Jesus' first words are of peace. A home that experienced fear and doubt now experiences the presence of Jesus. The phrase, "Peace be with you" is repeated twice. Were the disciples afraid and entertaining thoughts that Jesus would exact retribution for their lack of faith, denial and abandonment? These thoughts are not Jesus' thoughts. The reassuring greeting of Jesus signals that all is well. The cross has conquered sin; a new genesis is at hand.

Thirdly, it is in the home that the disciples receive their mission. After three years with Jesus they are about to be sent out on a mission to proclaim the forgiveness of sin through belief in Jesus the Christ. Closely united with their mission is the bestowing of the Holy Spirit on the disciples. Jesus not only gives the disciples a mission but he gives them the power to accomplish it. The Holy Spirit, which is the love between the Father and the Son, is now being poured out on the disciples. These once fearful disciples turn the world upside down and proclaim that everyone can have a relationship with God through Christ.

Finally, in the home, they receive the power to forgive sin. What a gift, to be reconciled to God and to each other, to be freed from the guilt and shame that sin brings and to receive the mercy of God. This power was given in the home.

✛ ✛ ✛

"WE COME TO A FULL SENSE OF THE DIGNITY OF THE LAY FAITHFUL IF WE CONSIDER THE PRIME AND FUNDAMENTAL VOCATION THAT THE FATHER ASSIGNS TO EACH OF THEM IN JESUS CHRIST THROUGH THE HOLY SPIRIT: THE VOCATION TO HOLINESS, THAT IS, THE PERFECTION OF CHARITY. HOLINESS IS THE GREATEST TESTIMONY OF THE DIGNITY CONFERRED ON A DISCIPLE OF CHRIST."

—Pope John Paul II, *Christifideles Laici*[29]

What can we take away from each one of these points? I think the initial action of Jesus appearing in the home sets the stage for the rest of the actions. If our homes are to become a domestic church, then Christ needs to be invited in; he needs to be present.

What follows is peace. A peace that the world can't give and money can't buy. This is a peace that only comes through the acceptance of the gift of the cross. For in admitting our sin, believing in Jesus and committing our lives to follow him, we can experience the inner peace and solitude for which we were created. Saint Augustine perhaps said it the best: "Our hearts were made for you, O Lord, and they are restless until they rest in you."

It is in our homes that we are formed and our gifts emerge. The Holy Spirit is at work in us from the very beginning of our existence. Each one of us is created for a mission, called to follow God in our lives. A great Catholic evangelist of the early twentieth century, Father Thomas A. Judge, recognized that the laity in particular had a mission. He formed them into cenacles, groups of laypeople who supported each other in faith and were committed to bringing the gospel into the workplace in the providence of their everyday lives. The order of laypeople he founded, the Missionary Cenacle Apostolate, has as its motto, "Every Catholic an Apostle." Many people thought that the involvement of the laity got legs after the Second Vatican Council, but Father Judge had the keen insight that there is an army of laymen and laywomen who are called to mission, whether married or single, first in their homes and then to their communities. Father Judge says: "It seems to me the Lord wants this family spirit.... I declare that I recognize the value of a family spirit, of a family working in the church, of a family with ardor.... I can see if the spirit is maintained, if the primitive spirit is passed down, this family idea will engender the most beautiful fruits for the honor and glory of God and for the edification of the church."

Our homes form us and attune our hearts to God's call. The way we pray, the moments we take for solitude, model to our children how to be in relationship with God.

The importance of forgiving sin in our homes cannot be overlooked. Christians must model the example of Christ. The humble, often difficult task of forgiving and asking forgiveness in our home will set the pattern for a lifetime. When we frequent the sacrament of reconciliation, we attest to the reality of sin in our lives. In receiving absolution for our sin we give witness to the saving love of Christ in the sacrament. Because of the encounter with Christ in the sacrament of reconciliation we are changed and so are our families.

Jesus continues to call men and women to mission, to be apostles. With the power of the Holy Spirit we can allow God to work in us and through us to bring about his kingdom, a kingdom marked by signs, wonders, forgiveness and peace.

PRAYER

Jesus, Son of God, bring your peace into our families and the families of our loved ones. Where there are fear and darkness, bring the light of your presence. Renew our hope and help us to discover the mission you have called us to. Breathe your Holy Spirit on us so that we may inhale deeply the richness of your love. May we be good and faithful servants all the days of our lives. We ask this through Christ our Lord. Amen.

REFLECTION QUESTIONS

1. Have you ever experienced the same fear the apostles felt in the upper room that evening?
2. Think back to a time when you experienced a supernatural feeling of peace. When did it happen? How did it feel?
3. Have you ever had an experience of the Holy Spirit in a personal way? How did that experience affect you?
4. Do you believe that you have a mission or calling from God? What do you believe your mission is?

CHAPTER CHALLENGES

- I will commemorate the feast of Pentecost by offering my words of peace and joy to someone I encounter.
- I will take advantage of the sacrament of reconciliation this week and thank God for the ability to encounter his forgiveness in this sacrament.
- I will pray to God and will ask the Holy Spirit to make the mission for which I was created clear to me so that I may follow God's call in my life.

CONCLUSION

Coming Back Home
(Ephesians 2:19–22)

So then you are no longer strangers and aliens, but you are citizens with the saints and also members of the household of God, built upon the foundation of the apostles and prophets, with Christ Jesus himself as the cornerstone. In him the whole structure is joined together and grows into a holy temple in the Lord; in whom you also are built together spiritually into a dwelling place for God.

I RECENTLY CAME BACK FROM WEST TEXAS WHERE MY WIFE'S FAMILY makes their home and where we had spent Christmas. My wife and daughter spent an extra week there with "Grampy and Nana," while I went back to work in the Garden State. Over Christmas each one of us "went down" as we called it, one after another, with a stomach virus. What touches one person really does touch a family! While I was at the airport, I was silently observing all the people in transit, some walking, some rushing, others sitting alone with earphones on and heads bobbing up and down, others juggling suitcases, food and children in tow, all

185

in transit. Most of them I gathered were going home after the holiday. Hopefully there were people waiting for them on the other side to welcome them home and embrace them.

Our hope as Christians is that we too will be welcomed home on the *other side*, if you will, into the loving embrace of our God and creator. In the meantime, we are living our lives as best we can in the providence of our everyday dealings with the joys, delights, suffering and hurts that affect us all. We don't go through this alone. Christ goes with us each step of the way. We have also been baptized into a community of believers who should support us on our journey of faith. The sacraments, the Word of God and the witness of holy men and women offer us spiritual nourishment and encouragement along the way.

In the midst of this we primarily live in families, whatever they may look like. Families that love each other, support each other, annoy each other, test each other, misunderstand each other and pray with and for each other. For better or worse our families are ours. There is never the ideal "perfect" family, but the hope is for a healthy family, one centered on Christ and his teachings, able to handle life as it comes to us.

Jesus spent a great deal of time in the homes and houses of the people we encounter while reading the Gospels. He impacted them for the better. It is my hope that in presenting some reflections on Jesus' presence in the homes that he entered our homes can be impacted for the better as well. It is a myth to believe that the Christian home is one of perfection. We all know the challenges that family living can bring us each day, even when we are committed to Christ and have a personal relationship with Jesus. I am convinced, however, that Jesus' presence in the home is the most important factor in having a healthy family; a family where prayer is the norm and where love and sacrifice are present in the small, ordinary things of life.

After being a teacher in the classroom for many years and engaging students and families from all walks of life, this has confirmed my suspicions; having a faith-filled family where Christ is present and worshiped produces faith-filled and joyful children who are equipped to face the world and its challenges and where they appreciate the gift of life.

In the passage above we are told that we are "citizens with the saints and also members of the household of God." Wow! What a statement. We are a family with those who have gone before us in faith. The Bible then is our family story in which we take our seat around the table. We are also reminded of the dignity each one of us has, for together, we grow into the holy temple of God, and God dwells within us.

It's not primarily what families *do* that make a difference, but it's who they *are* in Christ that shines through. Talking about prayer and actually praying with people are two very different experiences. I believe that Jesus can be just as present in our homes today as he was in the homes of his first followers if we allow him to enter. The reflection questions and chapter challenges are meant to help this process but are only a few ways to get the conversation started. I offer them with the hope that they will open some doors for Jesus to enter into your life, your home and most importantly, your family, so that you may experience the joy and love of Christ, a true presence of peace.

NOTES

1. *Compendium of the Catechism of the Catholic Church*, 337, http://www. vatican.va/archive/compendium_ccc.
2. Pope John Paul II, *Familiaris Consortio*, 26, http://www.vatican.va/ holy_father/john_paul_ii/apost_exhortations/documents/hf_jp-ii_exh_19811122_familiaris-consortio_en.html.
3. As quoted in Pope John Paul II, *Pope John Paul II: In My Own Words*, Anthony F. Chiffolo, ed. (Liguori, Mo.: Liguori, 2005), p. 65.
4. Pope Benedict XVI, Apostolic Journey to Cologne on the Occasion of the XX World Youth Day, Eucharistic Celebration, Homily of His Holiness Pope Benedict XVI, August 21, 2005, http://www.vatican.va/holy_father/ benedict_xvi/homilies/2005/documents/hf_ben-xvi_hom_ 20050821_20th-world-youth-day_en.html.
5. Pope John Paul II, *Redemptoris Custos*, 21, http://www.vatican.va/ holy_father/john_paul_ii/apost_exhortations/documents/hf_jp-ii_exh_15081989_redemptoris-custos_en.html.
6. *Catechism of the Catholic Church*, second edition (Rome: Libreria Editrice Vaticana, 1994, 1997), no. 534.
7. Vatican II Council, *Lumen Gentium*, Dogmatic Constitution on the Church, 31, http:www.vatican.va/archive/hist_councils/ii_vatican_council/documents/vat-ii_const_19641121_lumen-gentium_en.html.
8. Cardinal Joseph Ratzinger (Pope Benedict XVI), interview with EWTN News Director Raymond Arroyo, September 5, 2003, http://www.ewtn. com/library/ISSUES/RATZINTV.HTM.
9. Amber Dolle, quoted with permission of the author.
10. Quote attributed to Pope John Paul II.
11. Reverend Harold Drexler, quoted with permission of the author.
12. Melissa Dobbin, quoted with permission of the author.
13. Pope Paul VI, as quoted on http://www.bartleby.com/63/42/4242.html.
14. Prayer attributed to Saint Teresa of Avila. This translation is taken from http://www.carmelitedcj.org/saints/t_avila.asp.
15. Quote attributed to Saint Augustine of Hippo, http://en.wikiquote.org/ wiki/Saint_Augustine.
16. Quote attributed to Pope John XXIII.
17. Karen Schurtz, quoted with permission of the author.
18. Diane Wright, quoted with permission of the author.
19. Pope John Paul II, *Rosarium Virginis Mariae*, 31, http://www.vatican.va/ holy_father/john_paul_ii/apost_letters/documents/hf_jp-ii_apl_20021016_rosarium-virginis-mariae_en.html.
20. Pauline Von Mallinckrodt, *Prayers and Thoughts* (Mendham, N.J.: Sisters of Christian Charity, 1985), p. 67.

21. Pope John Paul II, *Reconciliation and Penance*, 5, http://www.vatican.va/holy_father/john_paul_ii/apost_exhortations/documents/hf_jp-ii_exh_02121984_reconciliatio-et-paenitentia_en.html.
22. Sisters of Mercy, *Thoughts from the Spiritual Conferences of Mother M. Catherine McAuley* (Dublin: M.H. Gill, 1946), p. 9.
23. Pope John Paul II, Message for a World Day of Peace, 8, http://www.vatican.va/holy_father/john_paul_ii/messages/peace/documents/hf_jp-ii_mes_08121995_xxix-world-day-for-peace_en.html.
24. Pope John Paul II, *Ecclesia de Eucharistia*, 1, http://www.vatican.va/edocs/ENG0821/_P2.HTM.
25. United States Council of Catholic Bishops, *Economic Justice for All*, 29, 1989, http://www.osjspm.org/economic_justice_for_all.aspx.
26. Pope John Paul II, Apostolic Journey to the United States of America and Canada, Meeting with the Young People of New Orleans, *Address of His Holiness John Paul II*, Louisiana Superdome Stadium, Saturday, 12 September 1987, no. 12, http://www.vatican.va/holy_father/john_paul_ii/speeches/1987/september/documents/hf_jp-ii_spe_19870912_giovani-new-orleans_en.html.
27. Von Mallinckrodt, p. 55.
28. Michael St. Pierre, M.C.A., quoted with permission of the author.
29. Pope John Paul II, *Christifideles Laici*, 16, http://www.vatican.va/holy_father/john_paul_ii/apost_exhortations/documents/hf_jp-ii_exh_30121988_christifideles-laici_en.html.